TICKET TO PARADISE

TICKET TO PARADISE

American Movie Theaters and How We Had Fun

John Margolies and Emily Gwathmey

Prologue by Harold Ramis

Ex Libris
Doris Toumarkine

A Bulfinch Press Book

Little, Brown and Company

Boston Toronto London

Dedication

In memory of Lisa Taylor, whose indomitable spirit and keen awareness of design will always be an inspiration to those of us who follow.

Photographs copyright © 1991 by John Margolies
Text copyright © 1991 by John Margolies and Emily Gwathmey

First Edition

ISBN 0-8212-1829-8

Library of Congress Cataloging-in-Publication information is available.

Some of the illustrations in this book are published with the permission of private collectors and institutions who are listed with the illustration credits on page 141.

The correspondence reproduced herein is used with the permission of the letters' authors; the letters have been shortened in many instances without indication that material has been cut.

Bulfinch Press is an imprint and trademark of Little, Brown and Company (Inc.)

Published simultaneously in Canada by Little, Brown & Company (Canada) Limited

Frontispiece:
Chicago Theater marquee, Chicago, Illinois.

Opening page:
Berkeley Theater, Berkeley, Michigan.

Book design by plus design inc.

Printed in Singapore

Authors' Note

Ticket to Paradise began with the photographs of John Margolies, who has traveled throughout the United States for the past twenty years documenting American commercial architecture. These unique pictures of movie theaters and drive-ins capture a significant tradition of design, much of which has disappeared forever from the landscape.

As a second element, Harold Ramis, Emily Gwathmey, and John Margolies conceived the idea of soliciting reminiscences from a cross section of friends and acquaintances, both in and out of show business. They felt that personal memories of actual experiences of being a part of the audience would enhance and add a meaningful dimension to the formal theater designs illustrated in the photographs. To broaden the spectrum of contributors, an Authors' Query asking for personal recollections and anecdotes was printed in the *New York Times Book Review*.

Postcards and other such ephemeral documentation of theater-related memorabilia are the third element included as part of the book. These fascinating bits and pieces of history, gleaned from the authors' collections, as well as from private sources throughout the United States, provide another important level of information about the moviegoing experience during its prime.

Acknowledgments

Special thanks to:

Those who took the time and effort to contribute by sharing their reminiscences and recollections about going to the movies.

Terry Hackford, our editor extraordinaire; Karin Fickett and Anita Meyer, for their stellar book design; David Naylor, for his authoritative research and books on the subject of movie theater architecture; Barbara Strauch, for her eagle eye and splendid judgment; Robert Heide and John Gilman, for their knowledge of movie memorabilia; and Angela Miller, for helping us to find Bulfinch Press.

Those organizations and individuals who helped to sponsor and underwrite the cost of the photography: the Architectural League of New York; Tom Bailey; Susan Butler; Asher Edelman; Rosalie Genevro; the Howard Gilman Foundation; Toni Greenberg; the John Simon Guggenheim Memorial Foundation; Agnes Gund; Ellen Harris; Barbara Jakobson; Philip Johnson; the Sidney and Francis Lewis Foundation; the Design Arts and Visual Arts Programs of the National Endowment for the Arts in Washington, D.C., a federal agency; the New York Foundation for the Arts; and Virginia Wright.

Those organizations and individuals who gave us access to their private collections of postcards and other ephemeral and historical materials: Donald Albrecht and Eleanor Mish at the American Museum of the Moving Image; Andreas Brown at the Gotham Book Mart; Frank Diaz at Pacific Theaters; Seymour Durst; Linda Laird of the City Planning Department of Hutchinson, Kansas; Marble Hill Historical Society, Columbus, Ohio; Don and Newly Preziosi; the Max Protetch Gallery, New York City; Guilford R. Railsback; Paula Rubenstein; John Sorensen; Eric Spilker; Joe Stamps; and Tom Todd.

TABLE OF CONTENTS

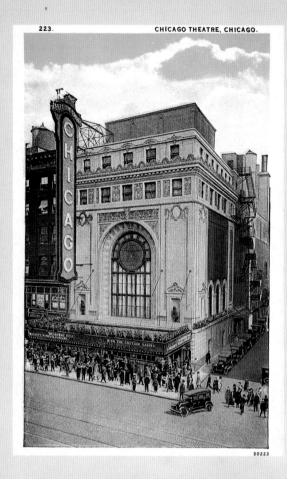

Chicago Theater postcard, Chicago, Illinois.
The Chicago was designed by Rapp and Rapp in 1921 and
was described as "the Wonder Theater of the World."

Prologue

It is 1954. I am ten years old. It is Saturday afternoon and my brother and I are walking to the Marbro Theater on the west side of Chicago. Or the Paradise. Or the Crawford. We will see two feature films, perhaps two serials, and at least five cartoons. The Brand brothers are with us, Earl, Lenny, and Burton. We make so much noise the usher separates us, banishing each of us to a different part of the theater. When he leaves, we sneak back to the balcony and reunite. We drop popcorn and empty candy boxes on the audience below us. We are not alone in this, as the entire audience is children.

Each cartoon gets a big cheer—Tom and Jerry, Sylvester and Tweety, Popeye, Mr. Magoo. The serials hold us spellbound and leave us hanging, eager for next week's episode of *Superman*, *Flash Gordon*, or *Don Winslow of the Navy*, then later *Don Winslow of the Coast Guard*. The movies themselves are mostly "B" Westerns and war movies. We refight World War II over and over, we fight North Koreans and Communist Chinese, we fight Indians, we fight greedy cattlemen and town bosses. And we always win. Why? Because we're the good guys.

Now it's 1960. We go to the movies at night now, Friday or Saturday. We go with girls. Or we look for girls. At the Granada, the Devon, the Uptown, the Howard—it's the same scene all over the north side. The arm slides around the back of the seat. The hand drops casually to the shoulder. Down the blouse to the swelling of the breast. Then she takes the hand and removes it. Not here. Later, on the sofa in her living room after her parents go to sleep. The movies are like foreplay. Monster pictures, science fiction, drama. We don't notice much. We are consumed by lust.

The theaters themselves we take for granted. The Granada, one of the great old-style movie houses done in Moorish splendor, stars twinkling in the huge domed ceiling, broad sweeping staircases, rococo detail on a grand scale. Downtown, the Chicago Theater, the State and Lake, the Oriental, each a miracle of design, like entering a temple or palace. Plush velvet everywhere. I would live in them if I could.

Now it's 1967. I finish college. I don't go to the movies anymore. I see films. I don't care where I see them as long as the film is foreign, obscure, or revolutionary, preferably all three. The big movie houses are dying. They close the Granada. It's the year of compatible color TV. I drop acid and go to Godard films. I want to act, I want to write, I want to have an effect. I want to stop the war. We're not the good guys anymore.

Now it's 1990 and I'm forty-five. I write, direct, and act in movies. It's still more fun watching them than making them. The theaters are smaller, screens are smaller, and business is better than ever. I rent movies on cassette and watch them at home on my VCR. Some say that videotape will kill the theatrical movie business, but I doubt it. There is still nothing that compares to sitting in a dark room with an audience and being bathed in that magical light. When a movie works, really works, it can take you like no other experience I know.

Some of the theaters pictured in this book are the baroque movie palaces of my memory. Others are the small town movie houses and drive-ins that we city kids never knew. Occasionally, perhaps on a car trip with my family, we'd pass through a small town and think how dinky everything seemed, wondering how those kids survived with only one theater in town. (Now I'm more experienced, having learned over the years to take movies however and wherever I can find them. I've been desperate enough to watch a Turkish movie with Greek subtitles in an open-air theater on an island in the Aegean.) Now I see video rental stores in every town and every mall. Nobody will ever suffer from lack of film again. The only loss will be these old theaters, where we all grew up together.

Harold Ramis
Los Angeles, California

Butterfly Theater postcard,
Milwaukee, Wisconsin, 1916.

BUTTERFLY THEATRE, Milwaukee, Wis.
Most Luxurious, Exclusive, Refined
Photo-Play House in America.
Absolutely Fireproof—Perfect Ventilation.
Change of Program Daily.
Complete Change of Air Every 3 Minutes.

NOW PLAYING

During the heyday of Hollywood, long before the advent of cable television, the "cineplex," and video stores, the ritual of going to the picture show was among the wonders of the world. Whether we watched movies in a monumental downtown showcase or at a more modestly scaled neighborhood house, the experience was transcendent and total.

During the three decades of the golden age—from 1913, when New York City's Regent Theater opened to become the first American movie palace, through 1946, the peak year in the industry's history with more than four billion tickets sold—moviegoing was nearly as much about where we went as what we went to see. Movie theaters were our most beloved icons, stimulating a full range of aural, visual, and even olfactory sensations. They insulated us from the ordinary. From street to screen, the magic of stagecraft was everywhere at work.

The entire experience of viewing a motion picture requires a suspension of disbelief; in fact, the very way we see film move is an optical illusion. Peter Mark Roget (of thesaurus fame) in the early nineteenth century observed that due to a quirky peculiarity of the eye, an image is retained for a fraction of a second longer than it actually appears. This so-called photographic memory of the eye regards pictures projected successively as being in continuous motion. Thus, the gigantic, extraordinary movie industry is founded upon persistence of vision—a strange, blinking, optical phenomenon.

David Crockett Theater postcard, Gatlinburg, Tennessee, circa 1945. Showing due respect to "Davey, the king of the wild frontier," the Crockett offered a welcome and coolness in this steamy tourist town in the Great Smoky Mountains.

"A World Premiere Night in Hollywood, California," postcard, circa 1940. The skies of Los Angeles came alive for miles around as banks of klieg lights circumscribed the heavens to proclaim another opening of another show.

Mayan warriors of cast concrete dominate the facade of the Mayan Theater in downtown Los Angeles, designed by Morgan, Walls and Clements in 1927.

Aztec Theater mezzanine postcard, San Antonio, Texas.

An ingenious architecture of illusion grew up to house the fantastic new invention called the movies. The buildings were ceremonial structures in which we could escape from reality into a communal yet anonymous space. Here we could be transported into a public yet somehow private dreamworld. Here, the rich and the working class could be swept away from ordinary time and place, together, as movie historian Ben Hall eloquently wrote, into "an acre of seats in a garden of dreams."

Whether we went to the movies downtown, crosstown, or just around the corner, the journey was filled with great expectations of a visit to the land of Oz. The names of the theaters themselves, etched in boldly lettered typography, pulsated with promise. Enchantment awaited at the Alhambra, the Bijou, the Majestic, the Oriental, the Roxy, the Paradise, or the Grand.

Early movie theaters protected patrons from harsh real-life reality by transporting them into an environment of present-tense time passing by in a darkened dream. Architect Thomas Lamb, who designed the Regent and other early Northeast palaces, believed that "to make our audience receptive and interested, we must cut them off from the rest of city life and take them into a rich and self-contained auditorium, where their minds are freed from their usual occupations and freed from their customary thoughts." And, as an opening night reviewer of the Regent observed, the "environment is so pleasing, so perfect in artistic detail, that it seems as if the setting were a prerequisite to the picture, that to an educated audience the two should, and must hereafter, go together."

The show itself began outside. Movie theater architects were pioneers in the promotional use of electric light. They designed broad canopies and towering animated marquees, wildly outlined in colorful tracer and chaser bulbs. Notices about attractions, coming attractions, and special events throbbed and undulated with promise. Blazing kliegs illuminating the skies proclaimed gala openings. A riot of electricity beckoned toward the Xanadu of a luminous modern pleasure dome.

Building facades were stylishly clad in an exotic spectrum of materials. Brightly colored compositions were made using several varieties of tiles: ceramic porcelain enamel; glass; and terra-cotta, a hard, waterproof, fireproof clay that could be intricately molded and colorfully glazed. Many other materials were pressed into service to create fanciful fronts, including brick, stone, stucco, and wood clapboard. Golden vertical towers made from molded metal loomed above adjacent shop fronts. Murals of purple and crimson depicted impressionistic fantasies.

A sense of ritualistic ceremony continued on street level at the gateposts to the kingdom of fantasy—the ticket booth, which was in miniature an architectural summation of the particular design palette utilized within. The ticket booth was the centerpiece of a composition of design refinements and details intended to add to the overall glamorous first impression. Colorful swirls of terrazzo tiles decorated the sidewalk beneath the marquee and led to doorways graced by snazzy railings and curvilinear glass. Elaborate frames encased the "lobby cards" describing feature attractions.

The lobbies of the early downtown showcase theaters were monumental antechambers designed to keep our minds off the fact that we were waiting. All manner of distractions could be found in the vestibules, foyers, lounges, stairs, waiting rooms, and promenades. Live birds chirped, while tropical fish swam about in ornate fountains. Marble statuary lined majestic stairways to mezzanines and balconies. Uniformed ushers led the way over plush carpet to cushioned, comfortable, clean seats. Perfume permeated the air of the snazzy powder room where polite attendants offered heated towels. When snacking became an integral part of the event, beginning in the smaller houses during the Depression, the array of sweets was staggering and larger-than-life. Just like the movies.

From 1915 through 1945, more than four thousand movie palaces—and countless smaller theaters, scaled down from the grander showcases—were constructed all across America. Every major crossroad in nearly every town

This small stained-glass insignia on the corner of the Warner Theater marquee in Erie, Pennsylvania (Rapp and Rapp, 1931) shows the care, elegance, and depth of design detail that was lavished upon this showplace.

Fairmount Theater postcard, Shaker Heights, Ohio, 1949.

RKO Palace marquee, Columbus, Ohio.

"Theatre Row at Night, Dallas, Texas," postcard, circa 1938.

A little girl enjoys a "Mutascope" (a form of peep-show machine) in this antique Austrian postcard.

and city in the country had at least one movie theater to call its own. Going to the movies had become our national pastime, and the growth of the industry coincided with revolutionary changes in American society, from rural and agricultural to urban and working class.

The evolution of the phenomenon of a theatrical building style — including a sense of procession, celebration, mystery, image, and memory — is linked with the miraculous development of moving pictures. During the nineteenth century, scientists, technicians, inventors, and entrepreneurs were obsessed with figuring out how to animate photography. The earliest results were viewed in "peep show" devices, at penny arcades or more elegant amusement parlors. After dropping a copper coin into a slot, you looked down into an opening similar to that of a stereoscope and turned a crank by hand. A light flashed on and you watched a continuous fifty-foot loop of one-inch film roll by, revealing a moon rising, a clown juggling, or the wiggle and tease of a belly dancer. The allure of these "living pictures" was instantaneous. Floods of pennies began flowing into hundreds of penny arcades all across the land.

When Thomas Edison unveiled his large-screen Vitascope machine at a New York City vaudeville hall in 1896, movies were transformed in America from a one-at-a-time event into a collective medium for the masses. Flickering black-and-white images ten times larger than life caused a sensation. Vaudeville became the primary outlet for this new two-dimensional marvel of silent moving pictures, a novel filler for the world of live entertainment.

Immigrant entrepreneurs, looking for a way up from their traditional trades, perceived the potential power and popularity of the movies. Makeshift storefront theaters, little more than a screen and rows of benches or uncomfortable chairs in made-over restaurants and retail shops, began to spring up everywhere. A sheet was hung on the wall; someone played the piano to drown out the noise of the loud projector; and excited patrons, many of them workingmen or newly arrived immigrants, read titles loudly to one another. Almost overnight these novel "nicolets," "nickeldromes," or most commonly "nickelodeons," so named in honor of their five-cent price, swept the country up in a form of delirium detractors called "nickel madness." In 1904, perhaps twenty-five nickel theaters existed. By 1909, eight thousand nickelodeons were packing them in across America. Six hundred of these were in New York City alone. These bare-bones storefront movie houses, the "poor man's show," or "democracy's theater," were the first showcases designed exclusively for the exhibition of "living pictures."

Before long, a dramatic change began to invade the size and social character of the audience. Entrepreneurs recognized that enormous profits could be made by enticing the middle class to the movies. Instead of employing grungy, poorly ventilated, overcrowded hotel ballrooms and unused lecture halls, they began transforming large-capacity legitimate theaters into movie houses where audiences could enjoy not only movies but the trappings of theatrical entertainment as well. By 1912, "small-time" vaudeville — a combination of film features and live presentation — had attracted a mixed crowd into these made-over theaters. The stage was set for the Regent, the Roxy, and several thousand other million-dollar palaces.

Production, distribution, and exhibition of motion pictures grew into an intense struggle to wrest control from Thomas Alva Edison, the first overlord of the movies. In 1908, he had established the Motion Pictures Patent Company, known as "the Trust," which gathered nearly all of the existing equipment patents together under a single corporation. Edison, whose actual contribution to film technology was relatively insignificant, along with his ten partners, announced that they alone owned the right to photograph, develop, and print motion pictures and that no license to do so would ever be issued to anyone else.

Growing resistance from the men who ran and supplied the storefront nickel theaters, together with a federal antitrust suit, finally toppled the monopoly in 1912; and by 1917, the Trust was dismantled by court action. During these

Theatorium postcard, circa 1912.

General Theater chain postcard, Chicago, Illinois, circa 1910.

Charlie Chaplin Studios, Hollywood, California, postcard, 1923. It is astounding to imagine that some of the greatest silent film comedies emanated from this rather humble line of residential-looking buildings.

Frontispiece, *The Union of Sound and Sight*, Western Electric Company catalog, 1929.

years of ongoing suits and antisuits, a large group of independent filmmakers and distributors entered the open market and set up production companies for themselves, many moving as far away from Edison as possible—to Cuba, Florida, Arizona, and California, where they had the advantage of year-round sunshine as well as distance from the Trust.

With the break up of the Trust, expanding nickelodeon profits, and a rapidly growing moviegoing public, many Eastern European Jewish immigrants saw a golden opportunity to give up their work in the jewelry and fur industries and enter the amusement business. They adapted the star billing concept from vaudeville and legitimate theater, and before long the public was writing fan letters to "the Biograph Girl" or "the Lone Indian." Since movies in neighborhood theaters and small towns were changed daily, to lure in the family trade, the demand for product and stars was open-ended. Providing inexpensive commercial entertainment was a necessary service and far more profitable than selling gloves. Industry profits and the quality of film steadily improved.

The two most successful showmen to emerge in the early days were William Fox and Adolph Zukor, both Hungarian Jews, who turned their attentions to audience expansion. If businessmen could make hundreds of thousands of dollars showing movies for a nickel to the lowest classes in American society, what could they make if everyone went to the movies? Fox captured the middle-class market by exhibiting films as half the program in large, established vaudeville theaters. This made vaudeville accessible to the working class and enticed vaudeville patrons to experience movies in comfortable circumstances.

Zukor experimented with the format and content of movies. To fulfill his slogan, "Famous Players in Famous Plays," Zukor presented an exclusive showing of Sarah Bernhardt in the full-length filmed play of *Queen Elizabeth* at the Lyceum Theater in New York in July of 1912. He charged one dollar for admission, a substantial leap from a nickel, both financially and psychologically. The French photoplay proved enormously successful in attracting the middle class to the movies. Immediately, a mad rush began to film popular plays and novels. It was clear that these full-length silent epics—particularly D. W. Griffith's 1915 masterpiece, *Birth of a Nation*, one of the most popular films in history—had somehow instantaneously propelled film into the realm of respectability. All that was required now was an equally cultivated setting in which to view the films. Only newly conceived and constructed theaters could provide exactly the right ambience. The theater business was changing: vaudeville circuit owners linked up with filmmakers and architects to create powerful studios capable of making and distributing movies within their own carefully constructed empires.

On the East Coast, Samuel L. Rothafel (Roxy) was the first great showman and supreme impresario of motion picture exhibition. His wild imagination led him to build playhouses for grown-ups, hybrid environments showcasing film, music, and live stage entertainment. "Don't 'give the people what they want'—give 'em something better" was the credo he employed in creating for the screen the legitimacy of the real stage, supported by a monumental theater building. Film rode to popularity on the recognized value of live productions and the status associated with architecture of heroic proportions.

The Regent was completed first, but it was Roxy's innovative management of the Strand that fixed the movie palace formula. When the Strand opened in New York in 1914, it "started a new style in motion picture theaters: comfortable seats, thick rugs, elegant lounges, velvet draperies, gilt-and-marble ornamentation—all the trappings of wealth that had previously belonged to a select few in the orchestra of a legitimate theater—and all for twenty-five cents," as described by Jack Possi in *Theater in America*. Recognizing the public's hunger for escape, Roxy created total environments for his audience. As he said: "Behind the theater there should be an idea, a *living* idea. Behind the programs there should likewise be an animate idea. It is that intangible something, that moving spirit, that makes the theater a *living* factor of local activities and a community center."

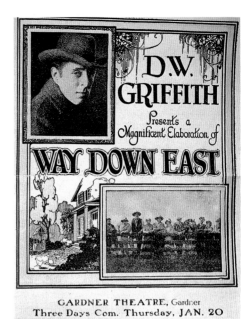

Advertising pamphlet for the Gardner Theater, Gardner, Massachusetts, circa 1920.

Strand Theater interior postcard, New York, New York, circa 1914.

15

"The Reward of a new Entertainment,"
The Union of Sound and Sight, Western
Electric Company catalog, 1929.

Out West in Hollywood, master showman Sid Grauman devised his own unique entertainment format. Movies were becoming bigger and longer, stars such as Douglas Fairbanks and Theda Bara were as popular and influential as royalty, and only specially constructed palaces were worthy temples in which to view their films. In conjunction with these lengthy, melodramatic, costumed film extravaganzas, patrons at Grauman's Million Dollar (1917) or Chinese (1927) theaters were treated to staged "prologues" thematically connected to what was playing on screen. If an Indian was part of the movie, an Indian theme was presented on stage as a kind of preview.

Along with other big-time film exhibitors, Grauman had recognized the need for a national network of theaters in which to distribute the wide range of movies that was now exploding out of Hollywood. A rush of theater construction utilized a wide ranging architectural palette. From the ridiculous to the sublime and beyond, anything was fair game. Conceived as showcases for silent motion pictures as well as live variety performances, designers were inspired by the neoclassical and beaux arts vocabularies much in evidence at the world expositions of the era. Influence came also from the European renaissance, baroque, and rococo styles, as well as from motifs of exotic cultures.

After the 1922 discovery of King Tutankhamen's tomb, Egyptian-style theaters were all the rage and could soon be found all across the United States. By the mid twenties, the art deco and streamline moderne styles, reflecting a collision of classical romance and machine age geometry, were very much in evidence in theaters ranging from small houses in seaside resorts to the breathtaking grandeur of Radio City Music Hall in New York.

The boom in movie theater construction created a new generation of architects. Their creations were glamorous, magical buildings of pleasure. They emerged on Main Streets from coast to coast at just that moment in time, after World War I, when we had become free and prosperous. There were new places to go, new products to consume, and lots of leisure time, all bankrolled by seemingly endless amounts of money to spend. Americans thronged to the movies in droves. Mothers whiled away weekday afternoons at palaces with professionally staffed nurseries and play areas. Children could hardly wait for weekend matinees, which soon came to feature serials and cartoons.

Thomas Lamb, a Scotsman who immigrated to America, designed more than three hundred theaters during his career. Stylistically termed "hard tops," these buildings were jazzed-up versions of opera houses and vaudeville theaters. Drawing on the influence of his European background and training, Lamb started traditionally by making extensive use of Corinthian columns, corner pilasters, marble balustrades, and other neoclassical elements. Over the years, working primarily for magnate Marcus Loew—whose motto boasted, "We sell tickets to theaters, not movies," and whose theaters offered Metro-Goldwyn-Mayer productions exclusively—Lamb's eclectic organization of detail expanded to include elements from Italian baroque, Louis XVI, Hindu, Persian, Chinese, and Spanish royalty. Among Lamb's most admired theaters were the Loew's Orpheum in Boston (1916), with vaulted ceilings painted in imitation of Josiah Wedgwood's pottery; the palatial Midland Theater in Kansas City (1927), which contained the first cooling, heating, and ventilating system of any theater in the United States; and Loew's 72nd Street in New York City (1932), Siamlike with Buddhas and magic lanterns, as well as five dog kennels to service its patrons' pets.

Working out of Chicago, enterprising exhibitors Abe Balaban and Sam Katz constructed an empire of wonder-theaters that turned the fledgling leisure time novelty of movie shows into the centerpiece of American popular culture. Working closely with architects Rapp and Rapp (the Rapp brothers, Cornelius Ward and George), Balaban and Katz cleverly located their temples of pleasure away from downtown, in crowded suburban neighborhoods accessible by mass transit and populated with immigrants yearning to become "American." George Rapp called the theaters "a shrine to democracy where the wealthy rub elbows with the poor."

Chicago Theater interior postcard, Chicago, Illinois.

Movie promotion postcard.

Grand Riviera Theater, Detroit, Michigan.

17—Interior Scene, the Tampa Theatre,

"The Pride of the South," Tampa, Fla.   121516-N

Interior postcard of the Tampa Theater, Florida. John Eberson designed the ornament-encrusted interiors of both the Grand Riviera (1925) and the Tampa (1926).

Designed to envelop the moviegoer in a transcendental vision of bliss — continuous organ recitals, elaborate stage shows, art galleries, crystal chandeliers, columned hallways, monumental stairways, triumphal arches, and other glittery artifacts of European high culture, including free child care and white-gloved ushers trained to treat audiences like royalty — the Balaban and Katz experience was a respectable refuge from everyday life, as awe-inspiring as going to church. The Central Park Theater (1916), their first, enticed summertime customers to escape the heat in amazing "air-cooled" comfort, a development hastened by experiments in refrigeration at the Chicago meat markets.

With air-conditioning, moviegoing became an even more popular year-round activity. Chicagoans of the twenties madly celebrated the opening of each new Balaban and Katz wonder-theater, marveling at the Chicago (1921), which crowed its name into an eight-story-high sign necessitating three thousand light bulbs. When the Balaban and Katz empire was absorbed by Adolph Zukor's Paramount operation in 1926, the Rapps' commissions expanded to include buildings from Portland, Oregon, to Paramount's flagship theater in Times Square in New York City (1926).

The pioneer of the ingenious "atmospheric" auditorium was John Eberson. Beginning with the Majestic Theater, which opened in Houston in 1923, the Austrian-born architect created indoor "stars and clouds" stage sets simulating open-air amphitheaters. Side walls were replete with windows; facades and rooftops were adorned with a plaster menagerie of gods, goddesses, hanging vines, stuffed birds, and mysterious statuary. Above it all twinkled a glorious moonlit sky and lazily drifting clouds, formed by a smooth plaster ceiling shell painted deep blue and pricked with hundreds of pinholes. The illusion of nature in an Italian garden, a Persian court, a Spanish patio, or a mystic Egyptian temple yard was intensified by an imaginative lighting system capable of coloring in sunrise to sunset. During a brief, seven-year span, Eberson designed and built a kaleidoscopic array of atmospherics large and small: from the giant Paradise and Avalon in

Chicago, and the Universal, Valencia, and Paradise in New York, to smaller but no less decorative theaters in Canton and Marion, Ohio, and Flint and Kalamazoo, Michigan.

Other architects working in the twenties included Greek-born Benjamin Marcus Priteca, who labored on the West Coast in conjunction with the Pantages chain and left his imprint on more than five hundred theaters. An early building, the Coliseum in Seattle (1916), an eclectic mix of classical and Oriental, was home to thirty canaries in its upstairs foyer. Priteca's most famous theater, the Hollywood Pantages (1930), was one of the first great art deco palaces and for many years was the glitzy setting for the Academy Award ceremonies.

The Boller Brothers, a firm that worked mostly in the Southwest, applied a whimsical Native American motif, pueblo deco blend, at the Kimo (1927) in Albuquerque, New Mexico, and encrusted the Missouri in St. Joseph with a Spanish baroque facade. C. Howard Crane, working out of Detroit, was the architect responsible for many of William Fox's showcases, including the four thousand-seat Fox in Brooklyn (1928), and the superlative five thousand-seat twin "Fabulous Foxes" in Detroit (1928) and St. Louis (1929).

The movies at these wondrous picture palaces were but a small part of a big show. Thirty-piece orchestras played at premieres. Huge Wurlitzer organs, played by talented musicians who became stars in their own right, created hope and depression with their thunderous sounds. Singers and dancers and other variety acts performed live onstage. Up on the screen, ponderous filmed versions of famous plays and novels were sandwiched between serials, Westerns, newsreels, short subjects, comedies, and sing-alongs.

In 1927, the introduction of "talking pictures" was the stupendous breakthrough that changed the entire face of the industry and made movies once again and forever popular. The Warner brothers—Harry, Albert, Sam, and Jack—who had worked their way up from nickelodeons and graduated into producing, premiered *The Jazz Singer* with its three Al Jolson songs.

Kimo Theater, Albuquerque, New Mexico.

Missouri Theater, St. Joseph, Missouri.
The Boller Brothers designed both the Kimo (1927) and the Missouri (1937).

Moviegoers raced to the talkies in droves, and the revolution was underway. Soon it was nothing but "all-talking, all-singing, all-dancing."

By the late 1920s, along with everything else, the movie theater boom began to go bust. So many had been built that there were suddenly not enough patrons to fill the seats. There seemed to be a dearth of creativity in the production of the movies themselves, which all too often were warmed-over potboilers used as vehicles to promote the career of one star or another. Audiences in the late twenties were beginning to be jaded. With the Great Depression, the movie palace era began to skitter to an end. Theaters became smaller and more efficient. S. Charles Lee was the most prolific and prominent architect of movie theaters of the art deco period and was dedicated to the notion that "the show began on the street." Lee set up shop in Hollywood, where he built or reconstructed more than four hundred theaters during the thirties and forties, mainly in California. Lee's first theater project, the Tower, in downtown Los Angeles, an exercise in compactness with a mere one thousand seats, offered the West Coast premiere of *The Jazz Singer*. In 1931, the Los Angeles opened, considered to be one of the very last picture palaces. It was a lavish French "barocco" building complete with restaurant, lounges, a nursery, a ballroom, and such innovative technical features as remote control switchboards, neon floor lighting along the aisles, and a periscope viewing screen in the lounge that Lee devised with the aid of an astronomer from the famed Mt. Wilson Observatory in Los Angeles. Lee's streamline moderne designs produced buildings that were pure "Hollywood," using materials such as etched aluminum, repousse detailing, glass brick, curved walls, and "black light."

During the thirties, while theater construction was diminishing, the art of movie-making was becoming increasingly more sophisticated. Plots thickened, production numbers multiplied, special effects dazzled. But still, in these hard times, Depression-era patrons had to be lured into spending ten or twenty-five cents for an afternoon or evening's diversion instead of on necessities such as food and clothing. Empty palaces required creative

General Electric air-conditioning advertisement, 1951.

marketing. The Roxy Theater built its very own miniature golf course out back so that customers could play a round of make-believe golf before losing themselves entirely inside. Managers gave away free china on "dish nights," held lotteries and gave away money and other prizes on "bank nights," and dreamed up a nearly endless variety of other promotional gimmicks to keep people coming back again and again.

Frankenstein promotion, St. Louis, Missouri, 1931.

The early 1930s also saw the development of a brand-new form of moviegoing, the drive-in movie theater. The first came about in the early 1930s, after a man named Richard Hollingshead, Jr., set up a projector mounted on the hood of his car and discovered that he could flash a movie on the side of his garage and watch it from the comfort of his front seat. Hollingshead developed and patented a ramp system enabling drive-in occupants to see over the roofs of their cars. On June 6, 1933, he opened the world's first "park-in" theater, in Camden, New Jersey. Admission was twenty-five cents per car, plus twenty-five cents per person, up to a maximum of one dollar.

A second drive-in opened in New England shortly thereafter, and by 1934, the first one had appeared in the "automobile heaven" of Los Angeles. At first the experience was pure novelty. Popularity would follow later, fueled not only by the compelling draw of movies themselves as an entertainment medium, but by the longstanding, all-American romance with the automobile as well. Now moviegoers no longer had to get all dolled up to go downtown.

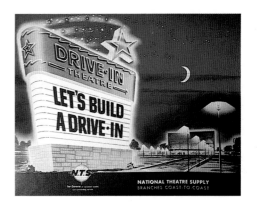

Cover of *National Theatre Supply* brochure promoting the construction of drive-in movie theaters.

At the first drive-in movie theaters, audio speakers were located on top of the screen tower, enabling everyone to hear and see, including the whole neighborhood. Soon, adjustable in-car speakers were developed, traffic circulation was figured out and perfected, screens were angled down to eliminate distortion, and a whole new realm of products was created, specifically tailored to the needs of the auto-viewing public.

What began in the 1930s as an oddity and a novelty gained nearly universal acceptance after World War II. This was the golden age of drive-in movie theater construction, paralleling the growth of highways and suburbs across the nation. By 1950, more than seventeen hundred drive-in screens loomed along the roadside landscape.

The drive-in movie theater experience in the United States had a relatively short life span. For about thirty years after World War II, people came back again and again to watch movies under the stars. But then the magic began to fade. The values and mores and the growth patterns of the environment that had created the drive-in also resulted in its falling out of favor. Land became too expensive to be used so wastefully. Families could sit at home and watch TV. Teenagers found other places to go to be alone.

Movie theaters have suffered an equally cruel fate. The very patterns that created the suburbs destroyed the old downtowns. As the population spread across the landscape, the old downtown shopping districts were bypassed by shopping centers located outside of town near the new suburbs. New, faceless movie houses popped up beside suburban parking lots, for those still devoted to seeing a movie in the theater.

As movie promoters had said for the past ninety years, movies are better than ever. The box office and theater attendance figures today are higher than ever, while many patrons are enjoying movies in the comfort of their homes, watching video store rentals or reruns on television.

Although most of the grand old movie houses from the golden era are long gone, a proud few still remain, cherished, saved, and restored. Some still show movies, but usually they have taken on a new role as the focal point of civic pride, and they serve new uses: as live theaters, performing arts centers, and concert halls. Although the movie theaters of our childhood are no longer operating on the street, they will live on in our minds and hearts forever, having transformed our lives, values, and visions of the world.

Drive-in theater sign,
West Boylston, Massachusetts.

State Theater tower and marquee, East San Diego, California. The State was a streamline moderne building dating from circa 1938.

Crest Theater tower, Fresno, California.

The Academy Theater tower, Inglewood, California, was designed by S. Charles Lee, circa 1940.

California Dreamin'

The designs of movie houses in California were state of the art. Not only was this the area where the movies were made and where the movie stars lived, it was the place that projected a dream life-style to the rest of the United States. Americans looked to the West to see their dreams and fantasies fulfilled. The cityscape of California was wide open and scaled to the rapidly moving automobile. And commercial development was escalating at a rapid pace just at the time the theaters were being built. All of these factors combined to produce the fanciest, most extravagant and exotic bunch of theater buildings to be found anywhere in the United States.

Esquire Theater, Sacramento, California.

The Fremont Theater, in San Luis Obispo, California, was designed by S. Charles Lee.

Culver Theater, Culver City, California.

Merced Theater, Merced, California.

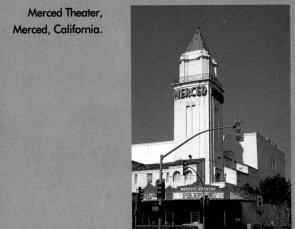

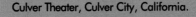

Balboa Theater, San Diego, California. The Balboa, designed in 1924 by William Wheeler, pays homage to the Spanish heritage of San Diego.

Loyola Theater, Westchester, California.

SCENE ONE
MOVIES MADE ME

Going to the movies used to be much more than two hours of idle entertainment. It was a passport to the whole wide world: exotic cultures; past, present, and future eras; and perhaps most important of all, exposure to hitherto unknown values and ethics. Moviegoing was a gateway to new ways of seeing and learning, influencing the most important choices we made—where we lived, what we did, and even how we related to the rest of the world.

A future poet, inspired by movie viewing at her "Midwest Chartres," dared to do more than dream of a life devoted to art. A black child growing up in Pine Bluff, Arkansas, experienced firsthand the pain and humiliation of segregation as he was forced to sit upstairs in the balcony of his local theater. And a young New Englander traded the pure pine air for the exhaust fumes and hubbub of Greenwich Village after being "fatally infected" by a movie whose title she no longer remembers.

Whether in the grandiose setting of Radio City Music Hall or in a humble edifice amid the cornfields of Minnesota, being part of a movie audience made us enlightened and responsible citizens of the adult world.

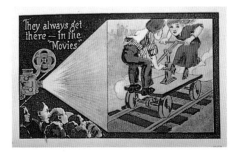

The Grandview
St. Paul, Minnesota

The Grandview was for me as a child in St. Paul in the 40s and 50s a kind of alternate cathedral, a cathedral where "fine arts" films were shown. I could, for example, see *The Red Shoes* there. The Grandview exists for me forever as a kind of counter-cathedral, a staging structure, a Midwest Chartres from which I—future poet—could launch out in *The Red Shoes* for places like London and Monte Carlo; in which I could hear Lermontov, the ballet director, say that the dance was more than poetry-in-motion, it was "a religion." In the hush of the theater, after contemplating the lit candle which would reappear at the end of the film, I was initiated into the glories and dangers of a life dedicated to art. The architecture of the Grandview provided space for contemplation of such fiery mysteries.

Deborah Larsen
Writer and Professor
Gettysburg College
Gettysburg, Pennsylvania

Highland and Grandview Theaters, St. Paul, Minnesota. Both of these sleek movie houses were designed by architect Myrtus A. Wright. The art deco Grandview was built in 1933, and it was remodeled in 1937 into a streamline moderne creation. The Highland has a cubist, brick moderne facade and dates from 1938.

Gem Theater, Claude, Texas.

THE MOVIEFAN FAMILY!
A GRAND SERIES OF MARVELOUS FEATURES IN EIGHT PARTS

SIERRA'S 280

The Capitol
Hillsboro, New Hampshire

Wide-eyed and remarkably innocent, as a child I loved to go to movies in the Capitol Theater in Central Square, Hillsboro, a desperate little mill town in south central New Hampshire. Central Square implies that there were other squares in the town; in fact, there were not, nor were there other entertainments. Not a bar in town, not a dance hall, not a pizza parlor—not in those days, the fabulous fifties. This was it for man, woman and child—the movies and an occasional minstrel show for which the town fathers would put on blackface.

In those days, my own father owned the local newspaper, which not only printed posters for the Capitol and advertised the shows weekly, but printed the tickets. Perhaps that's why my dad had a roll of them in the top drawer of his big oak rolltop desk—an enormous roll of salmon-pink tickets, more than I was ever able to use. Admission, then, was no problem.

Having saved the 15 cents, I had money left over for popcorn. Daisy Connor—to us kids, "The Popcorn Lady"—sold hot buttered popcorn afternoons and evenings from a little stand in the alleyway next to the theater. Of course I thought she lived in there, and the truth apparently is that she ran her stand for forty years; her husband, Lester Connor, ran a shoe repair shop next door. As I recall, the popcorn—sold in 5 and 10 cent paper sacks—was wonderful, and I retain a greedy enthusiasm for the stuff to this day.

Inside, the Capitol Theater was hushed and dark. Neon tubes glowed mysteriously, all was plush and carpeted. The floor sloped toward the screen and dark rows of rounded seats marched down a center aisle. We ate Jujubes from boxes. The music was loud, the whirr of the projector overcome by it, and then the show began. We always called them movies, and the first I ever saw was *Annie Get Your Gun*. "Anything you can do, I can do better," I yodeled to my brother for the next twenty years. Then I saw *Singin' in the Rain* and *South Pacific*. I would never go to the war movies, which played constantly and which the boys loved. Sensitive soul, I was led sobbing and screaming from *Lassie*.

It was in the movie theater that I got fatally infected by a longing for New York. I don't know what movie it was, but it was set on Bleecker Street and involved romance and Italian housewives hanging their laundry out the kitchen window. To me, with pine forest in my back yard and lungs full of fresh air, it was completely fascinating, imperatively desirable. I wanted sidewalks, pushcarts, Italian bread. I wanted neighbors, crowds, crime. I wanted New York—and not Park Avenue but Bleecker Street.

And I got it. The Capitol Theater closed in 1965, the projector was moved to the Concord Drive-In, and the premises were made into a restaurant which burned flat on January 21, 1990. Now I go to movies on Bleecker Street.

Cynthia Van Hazinga, Writer
New York, New York

Program cover, July 5, 1934.

Radio City Music Hall
New York, New York

Movies had become part of my family's lore before I was born. My mother, a music student, played the piano for the silents at an open-air theater to buy a Christmas gift for her future husband. When I achieved movie-going age, I became addicted to the glittering high-life of the cinematic metropolis, through which Carole Lombard, Irene Dunne, Cary Grant, William Powell, Kay Francis, Myrna Loy, Robert Montgomery, Jean Harlow, and Katharine Hepburn moved with such élan and panâche. When Fred Astaire and Ginger Rogers flew down to Rio and began their incredible series of hits, I was enraptured. This country kid from Covington, Louisiana, became determined to be an urbanite, definitely in New York and specifically in Manhattan, and lead the lives those magical images led.

Well, I finally did live in New York for twenty years or so, and thanks to those movie memories it has always been gilded with a little stardust for me, no matter what its real-life exigencies. I guess the movies of the 'thirties and 'forties somehow "set" me culturally or genetically or whatever it is they do, since I do not feel the same about San Francisco, where I now live, despite Clark Gable and Jeanette MacDonald and their earthquake and, later on, *Pal Joey*, *Vertigo*, and *Bullitt*.

On my first trip to Radio City Music Hall, I felt as though I was actually *in* an Astaire-Rogers movie set, as swell as any that Van Nest Polglase ever designed for the dancing couple. Waiting in the vast streamlined lobby to edge up the grand staircase, surrounded by gleaming metal, mirrors flashing faceted lights and reflections, enormous contemporary chandeliers, snappily uniformed attendants ("You're the pants on a Roxy usher," as Cole Porter wrote about that great house), and luxurious divans and carpeting, I could almost hear the strains of "The Continental" strike up. Then we could all sway in dance up and down the stairs and through the great space—led, of course, by me and my date as Fred and Ginger. Small wonder I had to find out more about how such wonders came to be, and unconsciously began to carve out a little niche for myself in the field of design.

There's a song in *Flying Down to Rio* titled "Music Makes Me." We used to snicker about this double-entendre as youths. But reworded a bit, it tells the story of quite a bit of my life: "Movies Made Me."

Jim Burns
Urban Design and Planning Consultant
San Francisco, California

Radio City Music Hall

In the early 1930s, when John D. Rockefeller, Jr., began building his commercial center in New York City, he chose S. L. Rothafel—known as Roxy—to lend his expertise as overall director of what was to be the largest theater in the world. Named Radio City Music Hall in honor of NBC, Rockefeller's star tenant, the theater was conceived by Roxy as a home for music, spectacle, and pageantry. Movies were but a minor aspect of his plan for this so-called Showcase of the Nation.

The building was designed of limestone by the Associated Architects, a firm that included Raymond Hood and Edward Durell Stone. The interior design commission was awarded to the artist Donald Deskey, who was just beginning to gain recognition for his creative use of industrial materials for decoration.

Opening night, December 27, 1932, featured a symphony orchestra, a ballet, the Roxyettes (to be renamed the Rockettes as the result of a legal battle), a choir, nineteen separate variety acts performed by the likes of Ray Bolger and the Flying Wallendas, an abbreviated version of the opera *Carmen*, a dual Wurlitzer console concert, and on and on and on. When the show finally ground to an end at 2:30 A.M., everything had been shown but a movie. The reviews the next morning of this overblown extravaganza were disastrous.

Nevertheless, Radio City Music Hall survived its opening night and went on to become a world-famous showcase for movies and stage shows, primarily on the basis of its sleek and extraordinary beauty. The more than 6,000 seats radiating out from a 144-foot-wide stage face a semicircular proscenium framed in fluted golden arches and draped with a golden contour curtain. The elegant simplicity of the Grand Foyer is a harmonious blend of mirrors and marble. Bakelite and cork enhance the coolly elegant color scheme of brown, beige, and gold. Statuary is cast in highly polished aluminum. Geometric moderne patternwork covers the interior walls, which feature a 40-by-60-foot mural rising high above the foyer's curving staircase. A visit to Radio City Music Hall, one of the few mythic survivors of the golden age, is still a ticket to paradise.

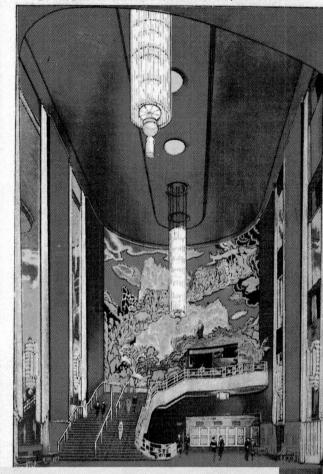

25 — FOYER OF THE RADIO CITY MUSIC HALL, NEW YORK CITY

44 — SCENE OUTSIDE RADIO CITY MUSIC HALL, N. Y. C.

6A-H2168

PUBLICITY DEPT.—RADIO CITY MUSIC HALL

The R.K.O.
New York, New York

I grew up in Manhattan. At five, I was allowed to go by myself around the corner to the R.K.O. on Broadway and 81st. There were no streets to cross. I was tall enough to stand tip-toe and push the nickel in to the cashier, who always leaned forward on his stool to examine the person attached to the fist with the nickel. The year was 1948.

As we passed through the lobby—which I don't remember; there was no reason to linger there—I would head for the children's section. Kids sat in the seats too close to the screen, off to the side, up front in the orchestra. This was the area ruled by the dreaded matron, white-uniformed, her grey hair pressed tight to her scalp by a net. She wielded a giant black flashlight. The beam moved relentlessly up and down the aisles throughout the movie. (It never occurred to me that she was so dour because her feet hurt.) Kids who talked got frozen in circles of blinding light. "Shush!" Her power over those rows was supreme; she could chuck you from the theatre. I never uttered a sound. I couldn't risk being sent away.

Years later, a grown-up eleven, I would drag my friends to the theatre early, pay the children's price (was it really already a quarter?), and lead the way to the ladies' room. When the coast was clear, we'd roll up our sweater sleeves, apply dimestore lipstick and pin our hair up. When the rest of the audience streamed in, we held our breath and climbed the stairs to the balcony. Sometimes it worked, sometimes it didn't.

Those glorious Saturdays and Sundays, the movies began around noon and lasted till twilight. First came the news, then a serial, then cartoons, followed by two features. We came out into the setting sun, bleary-eyed, dizzy and in the grip of a secret that none of the grown-ups hurrying down Broadway could share . . . a wonderful, unique, happy sense of having been away. It lasted exactly to the top step of my front stoop. The three flights of stairs up to the apartment were an ascent back into a world so much less real than where I had just been. The movies of my childhood were definitely my reality and my happiest memories.

Carol Hofmann
Los Angeles, California

Malco Theater, Pine Bluff, Arkansas.

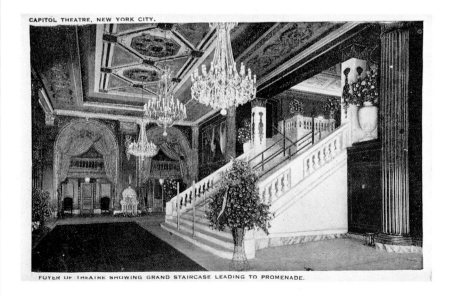

Capitol Theater foyer postcard, New York, New York, circa 1930.

The Malco and the State
Pine Bluff, Arkansas

Growing up in Pine Bluff, Arkansas, in the 50s and 60s was a combination of pleasure and pain. It was the segregated South and I am black. By law, and certainly by custom, all facilities were segregated, including the movies: whites at orchestra level, blacks in the balcony.

Now, the Malco Theater was on Main Street next to one of Pine Bluff's most exclusive dress shops, the location lending it an air of class and refinement. The State Theater, although located in a less upscale part of downtown and not as elegant as the Malco, was nonetheless another desirable movie venue. In both these houses, dreams became

reality; unthought-of places and things came into my senses. But the wondrous worlds unleashed in the dark were always marred by the dark reality of separation.

I remember that my chagrin at being consigned to the balcony was not for me, but for my mother—and the other adults. After all, my friends and I were children. And in the South, children, both black and white, were to be seen and not heard. My mother, no longer a child, was forced, along with her peers, to the upper reaches of these theaters because of race. So as we watched *Imitation of Life* together, I felt the hurt that made Peola want to "pass" (as white) as well as incredible sadness that some were forced to such a radical solution to ease their racial humiliation.

As the South slowly and unwillingly relinquished the burden of ignorance that sustained its racism, I was finally able to walk through the front doors. The significance of that first fearful entrance was not just an ingress into a movie house; it affected the collective existence of all Southerners and, for better or worse, created a plane on which a degree of equality existed. It signified that the house as well as the images on celluloid belonged to all of us. Without the complex drama of seating prerogatives and knowing one's place, the movies became what they always should have been, a vehicle for transport into worlds known and unknown.

Andrew Rowan
New York, New York

Blatt Brothers' Corry Drive-In Theater, Corry, Pennsylvania.

The Liberty
Mercer, Pennsylvania

"Going to the show" was one of the few things to do in Mercer, Pa. (pop. 3500) where I grew up in the 40s and 50s. This rural borough in Western Pennsylvania offered few visual or cultural amenities other than a rather pretty courthouse set in a square (locally called a diamond), a lot of lawyers, churches, a jail, and a very small public library. The Blatt Brothers Liberty Theater sat on the northeast side of the diamond in between Reznor's Jewelry Store and the Farmers Bank. I do not remember that it had any architectural character other than a marquee. I do remember what went on inside the theater. The movies changed every two days and because my mother was divorced (not the euphemistic "single parent") and worked, I was allowed to go to the show whenever I wanted and I went every time the show changed. The Blatt Brothers became one of my babysitters.

The first movie I ever saw was *Lassie Come Home*, which I saw with my grandmother. I can still see Lassie's bloody little paws making their way home over jagged rocks. I also vaguely remember going to see a film biography of Woodrow Wilson and weeping when he died. My mother told me no need to weep because "Mr. Wilson was a Democrat."

My favorite time at the movies was the Saturday matinee when for 10 cents you saw previews, a cartoon, a serial (usually Tarzan), a newsreel, sometimes a travelogue of the "as the sun fades in the west" sort, a Western and a grade B feature. Of course, nothing was grade B to me and my friends. Everything was AAA. I was born in 1938 and it seems unlikely that I was going to the movies much during WWII but I have vivid memories of the newsreels. They terrified me. I was sure Mercer would end up like the beleaguered European villages I was seeing on the screen.

The black and white Westerns and gangster movies were ok but I went to heaven when the big Technicolor musicals such as *The Harvey Girls* and *Meet Me in St. Louis* appeared. I cared nothing for plot or character development; what were they? What I wanted was a lot of music and glitz. Sonja Henie skimming across the ice in black and white was fine but Esther Williams and company doing water ballet was the ultimate thrill.

I still enjoy "going to the show" but it costs $7.00 and you have to watch advertisements and can't eat Milk Duds and popcorn because of your waistline and hips. The double feature has gone the way of the double header and no one ever swims or skates in the movies anymore. Talk about the end of the age of innocence.

Judith Holliday, Librarian
Ithaca, New York

The Mystic Theater, in Marmarth, North Dakota, was designed in 1914 by Guy Johnson. The stucco facade is dominated by an arched opening accented by a series of small light bulbs.

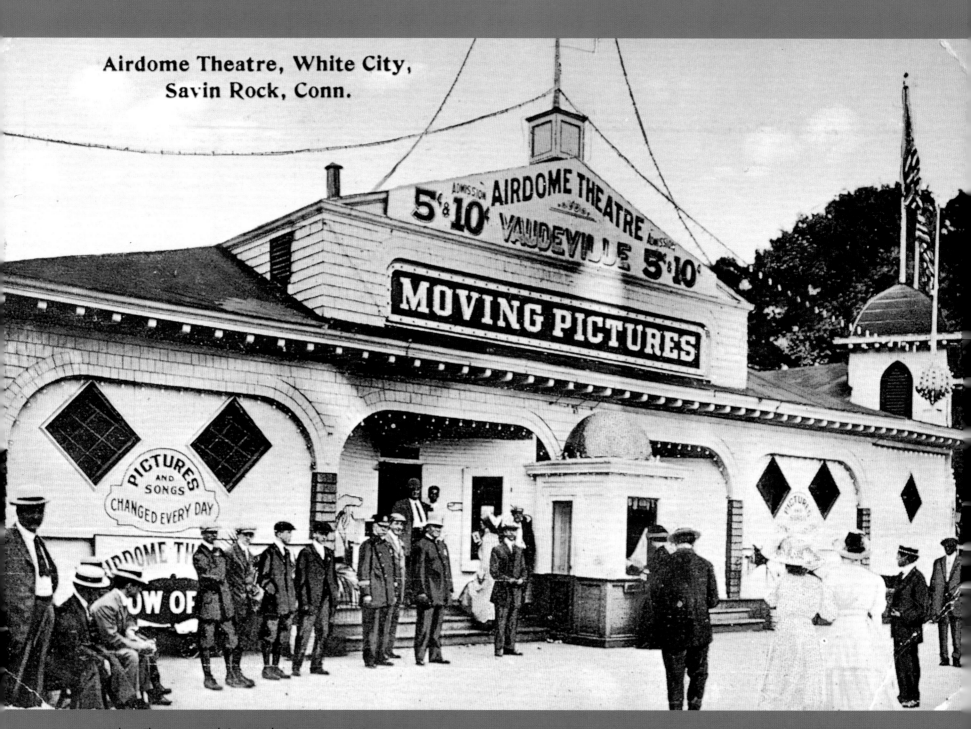

Airdome Theater postcard, Savin Rock, Connecticut, 1919.

SCENE TWO

THE GOOD OLD DAYS

With the technological sophistications of today, it is hard to comprehend that only yesterday movies were a marvelous new and primitive invention. Plotless silent film loops showed the world of still photography coming to life in flickering, jerky images. The addition of gradually longer and increasingly more complex stories, accompanied by live piano or organ music, enhanced vaudeville shows. By the end of the 1920s, sight and sound had inevitably been combined on screen, and Technicolor was just around the corner. The whole experience of going to the movies was now played out in opulent picture palaces every bit as exotic as the epics and spectacles up on the screen.

Twin brothers remember seeing their first movie in 1910, an animated, blurry image on the wall of a tavern in Coney Island. In the 1920s, a farm girl from Massachusetts anticipated her emotional reactions to silent movies by listening to the rhythm and intensity of the opening musical accompaniment. For many devotees, serials were the best part of all. These forerunners of soap operas, often fifteen or twenty installments long, required religious attendance in order to keep up with heroines in distress, heroes on the brink of disaster, and villains plotting one dastardly deed after another.

Within three decades, movies had evolved from *The Great Train Robbery*, the first movie to tell a simplistic story within a few brief minutes; to D. W. Griffith's *Birth of a Nation*, a grand epic with a cast of thousands which went on for three hours; to *The Jazz Singer*, the first feature movie to synchronize speech, music, and sound effects—with Al Jolson crooning "My Mammy" to an astounded audience of millions.

DOUGLAS FAIRBANKS
TRIANGLE STAR

The Bijou

Ashburnham, Massachusetts

In the 20s when I was a girl, we lived on a farm about
three miles from the nearest movie theater, the Bijou, in
Ashburnham, Massachusetts. On special Saturdays we—my
brother and two sisters and an occasional farm boy
neighbor—would walk to town to see the show, which
probably cost us 10 cents apiece. In the theater, we
would sit quietly waiting for the piano player, a
talented woman, to walk down the aisle. Only then would
the movie begin. We would listen closely to the music. If
it was rather soft and quiet, we knew we had to be sad or
attentive to the love scenes. When she really banged
away, we would get excited and noisy, waiting for the
Indians or the enemy to appear.

How we loved the serials. I remember *The Riddle Rider*,
and how we hoped never to miss a part. Douglas Fairbanks
was a favorite in fairy tales, *Sinbad the Sailor*, and in
costume dramas. My own favorite was Ramon Navarro in
Where the Pavement Ends, *Romance Begins*, with a scantily-
clad native beauty in a sari.

Today the Bijou Theater is owned by the Odd Fellows, and
the Ashburnham Grange also uses it for meetings. I'm told
there are a few posters still left in the basement.

Sylvia Van Hazinga, Retired Teacher
Peterborough, New Hampshire

(Geo. Bey, Jr., Pub.)   THE BIJOU THEATRE, ATTICA, N. Y.

These two postcards of another "bijou," in Attica,
New York, demonstrate its elegant evolution during
the decade from 1910 to 1920.

1917
PROGRAMME
OF
Savoy Theatre
South Paris Maine.

For the Week Beginning

May 7th

SAVOY PRINT

WEDNESDAY NIGHT

METRO
One Million
Dollars

In 5 Reels
Featuring
William Farnum

Latest Selig News

6 REELS OF PICTURES

THURSDAY NIGHT

BLUE RIBBON FEATURE
Reverend Cyrus
Townsend Brady's
Island of
Regeneration
6 REEL FEATURE
Produced under the Personal
Supervision of J. Stuart
Blackton and Albert E. Smith

For Value Received,-Comic

2 FULL SHOWS

7 - REELS

FRIDAY NIGHT

Bargain Night
Knickerbocker Star Feature
PAY DIRT
5 Reel Western Feature
Featuring
HENRY KING

A Lesson
in Labor
IN 2 REELS

THE STONING
In 3 Parts
Featuring
VIOLA DANA

10 REELS

SATURDAY NIGHT

Chas Chaplin
Marie Dressler and Others
in
Tillie's Punctured
Romance
In 6 REELS

2nd Episode of
The Serial Sensation
THE CRIMSON STAIN MYSTERY
Featuring
Maurice Costello and Ethel Grandin
16 Episodes   2 Reels Each

2 Shows 2

8 - - REELS - - 8

Theater program, 1917.

The Palm Theatre, Leavenworth, Kas.

Play being shown at the Palm Theater, Leavenworth, Kansas, in 1909. This long-forgotten drama had a plot revolving around a moving picture theme.

The State Street
East St. Louis, Illinois

I am eighty-three years old, and I remember the silent movies when I was five years old. The neighborhood theater was named the State Street. The cashier was seated in a dimly-lit hall and admission was 5 cents. An elderly man was seated at a piano playing Tin Pan Alley music while the actors and actresses were jumping around on the screen.

Each week, there was a box near the entrance, with numerous cardboard pieces of something like a jigsaw puzzle. It was an octopus. They let people take a piece each time they went to the movies, and in a period of six months if they completed the whole octopus the prize was close to $100. My mother went every week, and at the end of six months all she had was a bunch of octopus legs.

Marnella Cunningham
Evanston, Illinois

MY DARLING BABY:

TONIGHT I SAW A MOVIE THAT REMINDED ME
OF OUR LOVE AND MADE ME SO LONESOME FOR YOU
I COULD NOT RESIST WIRING YOU STOP I HAVE
BEEN THINKING ABOUT YOU CONSTANTLY STOP LIFE
WITHOUT YOU IS SO EMPTY STOP I HOPE THAT
SOME DAY SOON WE WILL NEVER HAVE TO BE APART
STOP PLEASE WIRE ME THAT YOU ARE LONESOME TOO

YOUR LONELY

—W—

Interior of Moore Theater, Seattle, Washington, 1909.
The movie projector in the foreground of this postcard proves that
even at this early date, the Moore was showing motion pictures.

Lyric Theater box office, Logan, Utah.

Proctor's Theatre, Troy, N. Y.

The Theaters of Troy, New York

The nine-mile stretch of the city of Troy, New York, had by the mid-1930s at least nine movie houses. From North Troy to South Troy there were the following theaters: Lansing, Bijou, Troy, Griswold, American, Proctor's, Rose, Madison and Monroe. Seating from 200 to 2,500 these flicker monuments to Thomas Edison seated the fans on bone-bruising seats or plush-covered springs.

Here in Troy in the "Roaring Twenties" we had our own ornate movie palace — Proctors. It regularly billed vaudeville acts (George Burns/Manny King) and a movie. The Troy had its classical orchestra under the direction of T. Roy Kiefer. Proctors and the American still survive. Proctors is idle, and the American shows only idylls of sex.

The Proctor had a third balcony dubbed "the spits"; admission was only 15 cents. The heavenward-perched seats in "the spits" were close to the source of the picture. The projector noise was inescapable. But we were easily transported by a movie spectacle just as were those down below in the 35-cent upholstered seats.

My friend Norman and I were in balcony seats to view the thriller *King Kong*. There was the added excitement of watching lovely Fay Wray in the hands of that out-of-this-world-sized gorilla. There was an acrobatic costumed gorilla who at intermission swung out over the audience and raced across the balcony rail. We all screamed. It was some show, but it was not enough to distract us over coffee afterward from talking about Fay Wray.

Edward J. Keyes, Retired Engineer
Troy, New York

41

The Omaha was once the World, and in its salad days it was described as that city's "finest playhouse." By the late 1970s, it stood forlorn and deserted, and it was later torn down.

The Court
Auburn, Indiana

The Court Theater did not have an imposing facade, although the marquee was of the usual informative and "protective" design. However, the slight rise in the entrance flooring brought patrons up to the rear of the raked seating area, and induced a mood of great anticipation. One paid, ascended, and entered at the rear of what was to a child a fairyland or at least a trip to the Faraway Places of story books. It never entered my mind that the Court might have been named for the fact of its site opposite the Court House. The real reason seemed obvious: the theater patron entered an exotic *courtyard*—of balustrades, beige stucco walls pierced to reveal enchanting alcoves, vistas festooned with ornate balconies, and great vases filled with what were understood to be lush floral arrangements. All was softly lit in front, with the beige tonality warmly inviting and reassuring, while we waited for the movie to begin. More wondrous was the back-lighting of blue as the deep, gorgeous tint illuminated the farthest wall of blue while the overhead sky also shone richly blue, with twinkling lights in abundance. Overhead, this arched ceiling was truly a Far Eastern night sky; the twinkling lights were stars transporting us quickly into a world of imagination quite removed from the town's nearby cornfields. When the warm beige of the houselights went off, a romantic and mysterious blue remained. We could hardly wait for the show to begin.

I don't remember all of what we saw in the days of silent black and white movies. I don't even remember the ambient organ music, except that my mother—our accomplished church organist—filled in once. The music was, after all, only secondary and taken for granted. We expected to hear at appropriate times the soft or thundering chords, or to be whetted by the music of anticipated terror.

Many years later, while I was in college, I recall attending some summer stock production at the Court, along with a college classmate. By then (the late thirties) I was older and the magic was gone. World War II was upon us. There seemed to be an incredible amount of dust on the fake bouquets in the vases. The show and the general ambience seemed pedestrian. The size and scale of the building—inside and out—seemed small and insignificant. All the decor seemed dated, worn, pretentious—even ridiculous. I wouldn't have opted for "modernizing" the Court, however; by that time I was majoring in art history and my appreciation of architectural history included Art Deco, and other Auburn, Indiana, styles.

I don't know what changes have come to this typical little theater. The outside never was a great wonder. In any case, I do sometimes think back to the innocence and romance of the Saturday matinee in that small town. Sunny day or not, we crept softly into the darkness, past box office and usher, to find our seats in the Court. The soft lights bathed the stucco facades in golden beige. As lights slowly dimmed our voices dropped and we whispered in wonder and excitement. Only the blue lights and twinkling stars remain . . . and in the romantic courtyards the vases grow to Ali Baba size.

Eleanor Ferris, Retired Educator
Amsterdam, New York

Astro Theater, Omaha, Nebraska.
The Moorish-style Astro, once called the
Riviera, was designed by John Eberson
in 1927. It was closed in the 1980s.

RIALTO—AMERICA'S MOST BEAUTIFUL MOVING PICTURE THEATRE, 15TH AND DOUGLAS STS., OMAHA, NEB.

Old New York

The first movie I ever went to was in 1910 with my Uncle Ike, who took me and my twin brother down to Coney Island. After parading up and down and looking at the wonders of all of Coney Island, we stopped in at a beer joint of some kind, and while we were sitting there, saw a movie being projected on a screen at the other end of the establishment. I remember it distinctly because the movie was very confusing to me. I have a faint recollection that it was supposed to be about the French revolution, and you can imagine what transpired with guillotines, etc. For a six-year-old, it was not only mesmerizing but especially scary. This was pretty nearly at the beginning of all the motion picture activity. And so this whole affair was rather primitive.

By the time we were ten we went to the neighborhood theaters, which abounded in the section of Brooklyn in which we lived. Like all the rest of the kids of that time, we had a Saturday afternoon matinee that practically all of our friends, and, of course, all of my brothers and sisters, went to religiously. Piano players provided accompaniment because there was no sound. All was in black-and-white. The movies I remember most were the serials, and we used to stamp, whistle, holler, cheer, clap, and do everything possible to urge on our hero or heroine. The movies were the Pearl White scenarios, which were full of excitement of the usual kind: the gal being tied to the railroad track or the car falling off the cliff. Then came *The Broken Coin*, *The Iron Claw*, and, a little later on, *The Mark of Zorro*. I remember the breathless anxiety with which we waited for the next episodes so that we could see what happened.

Jerome Franks
Cincinnati, Ohio

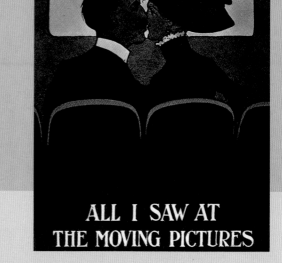

The Star
New York, New York

Back in the 1920's we used to pay only 5 cents to 10 cents to see a movie. If you did not go with your parents, they would not sell you a ticket. You had to be at least eighteen years old to buy your own. So, every week we kids had to go wait by the ticket window until we found someone who would buy us one. The Star opened at 12:00, but we had to get there early if we wanted to get lucky. Sometimes people would be so nice that they would buy ten to twenty tickets so all the kids could enjoy themselves. I always had to wait with my older brother; that's the way my family wanted it.

It seemed like every time we got comfortable waiting for the picture to begin, the movie camera would break down. All the kids would start hollering and booing the camera operator. I loved to hear the piano player keep up with the picture. It was by watching the eyes of the actor or actress that you could tell what they were supposed to be thinking and what part they were playing. And the serials were what the movie house used to make sure the kids would come back. They would show a serial that always had about fifteen to twenty parts and you had to go and see every part. The end of each part always put you in so much suspense that if you missed the next week, you had to ask one of your friends how it ended or what happened.

After many years of pictures with no sound, it sure was a great day when I had a chance to go and see the first talking picture, with Al Jolson, *The Jazz Singer*. After that, everything seemed to change with the movie business. Even the prices started to go up.

Daniel Chomiw
Holiday, Florida

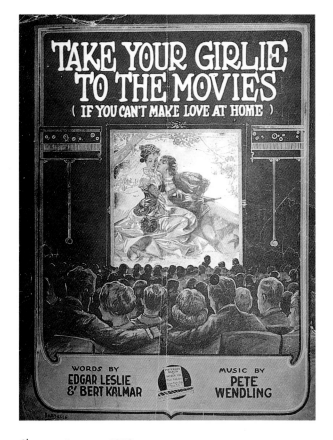

Sheet music cover, 1919.

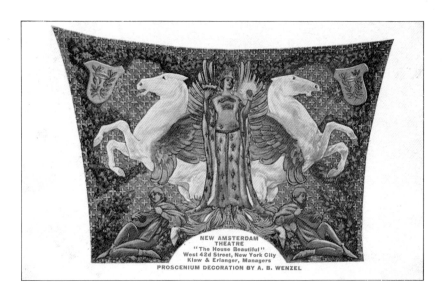

Proscenium decoration postcard,
New Amsterdam Theater, New York, New York, circa 1905.

Strand Theater lobby, New York, New York.

New York in the 20s and 30s

Silent films were first introduced to my entertainment world before the Great Depression. As a young entrepreneur, age six, I raised money to attend the Forest Hills Theater in Queens, New York, in a unique way. I sold tickets to my school friends to visit my Grandmother Lewis, who was missing a finger. My classmates were intrigued with the story of a cut from a rusty kitchen knife and the gangrene which set in necessitating amputation. I charged my customers 5 cents to shake my grandmother's hand.

When I raised enough money for a 25-cent theater ticket, I would walk around the corner and pay my fare. The sight of the large marquee with bright lights excited me. One of my favorite motion pictures was *Fu Manchu*. An organ played during the performance. The music became very intense during a melodramatic scene. One such picture showed the heroine strapped by the villain to the railroad track. When the hero rescued the fair maiden, the music changed to a romantic tune.

The Forest Hills Theater had an art deco lobby, velvet seats and a blue and gold decor. To me, it was like stepping into another world of fantasy. The only drawback were the boys in the balcony with bean shooters. They aimed at the girls in the orchestra seats and the organist when he stood to take a bow. Spit balls were also popular. A matron in a white uniform tried to keep order, but only succeeded in becoming a target. Although the films were silent, the audience was not. Ushers in uniform led you to your seat.

Once a year we visited Radio City Music Hall on Fiftieth Street in Manhattan. Here the audience behaved with decorum. I will never forget my first view of the golden circular staircase with the mural on the wall entitled "The Author of Life," by Ezra Winter. Programs were passed out describing the art. The stage was a block long and had radiated lights in brilliant hues. Boxes lined the side walls of the auditorium. People came from all over the nation and the world to view this elegant showplace and to see the famous "Rockettes."

Another fabulous theater we enjoyed visiting was the Brooklyn Paramount. This theater was truly a palace, with its French Baroque decor. All the Rock and Roll set gathered here for fabulous shows in the '50s.

Loew's Kings was another fabulous entertainment hall. It was located on Flatbush Avenue in Brooklyn, New York, near Erasmus Hall where I attended high school. Whenever I had an afternoon free of classes, I would call my mother to meet me there or go with friends. The theater was designed by Rapp and Rapp and opened in 1929. A terra cotta entranceway formed an arch into the grand lobby. The Greek columns were elegant. Barbra Streisand, a student at Erasmus Hall High School, ushered there. Here she may have been inspired to go on stage. I remember the mirrored walls in the lobby. You felt like you were entering another world when you visited Loew's Kings Theater. It held thousands of spectators. On a Saturday night date, this was the place to go. Today TV and tapes on VCR are taking away the pleasure of going to a movie theater. Many a romance has begun with holding hands during a show or stealing a kiss in a drive-in theater. Sitting at home in front of a TV will never take the place of an evening at the local theater.

Virginia Lewis MacInnes
Forest Hills, New York

Audubon Theater, New York, New York. In 1912, arcade and nickelodeon operator William Fox hired architect Thomas Lamb to design a two-story building combining a theater, stores, offices, and a second-floor ballroom. For the full-block site at 166th Street and Broadway, Lamb used plain brick on one side but wrapped the rest of the structure with a polychrome terra-cotta facade topped by a projecting cornice. The Audubon has been through many transformations since its gala opening, including a stint as the Beverly Hills and, soon after, as the San Juan. In 1965, Malcolm X, the Black Muslim leader, was assassinated at a rally in its ballroom. The Audubon still stands in 1990 but, sadly, is slated for demolition — to be replaced by a medical center.

Grauman's Chinese Theater,
Hollywood, California.

SCENE THREE
UPTOWN/DOWNTOWN

By the 1930s, America had been swept away in a mad movie mania. The fantastic production numbers presented on the screen were often surpassed by the movie theaters themselves. Their names still ring like magic—the Roxy, the Paramount, Grauman's Chinese and Egyptian. . . .With much pomp and circumstance, and loads of ruffles and flourishes, the experience of going to the movies was a spectacle unto itself. The exceptional was the norm.

For the little girl growing up in Atlantic City, a very special movie theater with stars twinkling in the sky of its ceiling was more magical than the boardwalk with all its temptations. A woman from Tennessee recalls avoiding World War II "blackouts" as a young girl by seeking sanctuary in her local theater. An artist who grew up going to Grauman's Chinese remembers best a machine that for a quarter dispensed a miniature replica of the theater itself, in hot colored wax.

And so it went in cities large and small, with packed audiences everywhere. Carrara marble statues of European royalty and Greek gods, bigger and better than the originals, looked on benignly as awed patrons roamed through dazzling lobbies into equally ornate motion picture halls. The theaters themselves were houses of magic; everything was larger than life. Just like in the movies.

Grauman's Chinese Theater

The exotica kingdom of West Coast showman Sid Grauman—including the Million Dollar, the Metropolitan, and the Egyptian—was crowned in May of 1927 with the opening of his Chinese Theater, designed by architects Meyer and Holler. Perhaps the best known of all the picture palaces, and still one of the biggest stars in Hollywood, this kitschy homage to the Orient featured a complex system of pagoda roofs, marquees topped with carved silver dragons, crimson antique rugs, wax figures of mandarins and ladies of the court, and troupes of ushers dressed in authentic Chinese costumes. High above the gigantic forecourt, which was originally lined with rare tropical trees and cocoa palms, an authentic Chinese gong notified patrons that the show was about to begin. The sidewalk of the courtyard became famous in its own right when a star visiting the construction site accidentally stepped in wet cement. The tradition of autographed concrete handprints and footprints of the stars caught on immediately and remains a popular tourist attraction to this day.

Grauman's box office.

Grauman's Chinese
Hollywood, California

I grew up in Los Angeles. The most memorable movie house for me was the Grauman's Chinese, in Hollywood. I wasn't impressed by its gaudy interior. I knew it wasn't a real Chinese temple. I wasn't excited by being able to match my kid's hands and feet with Shirley Temple's marks in the cement out front. What I liked was the wax injector machine just to the side of the theater. Everybody'd be trying to fit into John Wayne's cowboy boot indentations and I'd be slipping quarter after quarter into the machine that gave you a tiny version of the Grauman in hot colored wax. It smelled good, like melted crayons, and plopped into your hand, warm and pliable.

The other great thing about the theater was the women's bathroom. I had never seen anything like it. I got to use it all by myself when my parents took me to see the movie Exodus. I don't remember much, just that my mom and dad brought their own box of Kleenex to the theater. I guess someone told them they'd be crying a lot. In the bathroom, right after the movie, a whole line of sobbing women waited their turn while secretly peeking into the huge mirror to check how they looked.

I still have a couple of wax models of the theater. It's strange, but the wax dummies look a lot more real to me than the theater ever did.

Ilene Segalove, Artist
Venice, California

WORLD PREMIER. GRAUMAN'S CHINESE

T108   HOLLYWOOD, CALIFORNIA   63799

Indiana Theatre, Terre Haute, Ind.

Blackouts in Knoxville, Tennessee

During the Second World War, when I was between the ages of
eight and ten, living in Knoxville, Tennessee, my parents would
make a special but not festive ritual of taking us to the movies
on the nights that the city declared "blackouts." Blackouts were
when no lights or candles or match flames or log fires were
allowed. Black cloths would be hung on the windows. The air raid
wardens would then patrol the streets all through the city to
"practice" for any eventual invasion.

Anyway, we would get dressed up and go to the fancy movie house
on Gay Street. I've forgotten the name of the movie house, but
to a young girl it was so glitzy and sparkled and so elaborate
that it made me feel like I never felt anywhere else. I recall
these blackout nights vividly.

Angela Gorsuch
St. Simons Island, Georgia

The facade of the Indiana Theater, shown in a 1930 postcard
and a 1980 photograph, has been transformed by time, losing
much of its wedding cake ornamentation.

THE PALACE THEATRE, CANTON, OHIO

Palace Theater box office.

The Palace Theater in Canton, Ohio, was designed by John Eberson in 1926 and has stood the test of time. It has been restored and now serves as a performing arts center.

The Roxy
New York, New York

When I got to be around thirteen or fourteen, the marble palaces like the Roxy, the Paramount at 42nd and Broadway, and others came into existence. They were really breathtakingly ornate. The ushers were all dressed up in very fancy uniforms. They patrolled the aisles and seated the audience with a great many flourishes. You didn't have the ordinary peanut and popcorn stands of today, but counters which dispensed refreshments in the form of fancy candy and the like.

I remember distinctly the first time I walked into the Roxy with my father and brother. The enormity of that lobby, with the main staircase that flowed up to what seemed to me the sky, was really overpowering, to say the least. And then, after you got into the theater and got seated, the show would get ready to start, and the organ would come out of nowhere, really out of the pit, with a very good organist playing. It was pretty impressive stuff to a youngster.

Jerome Franks
Cincinnati, Ohio

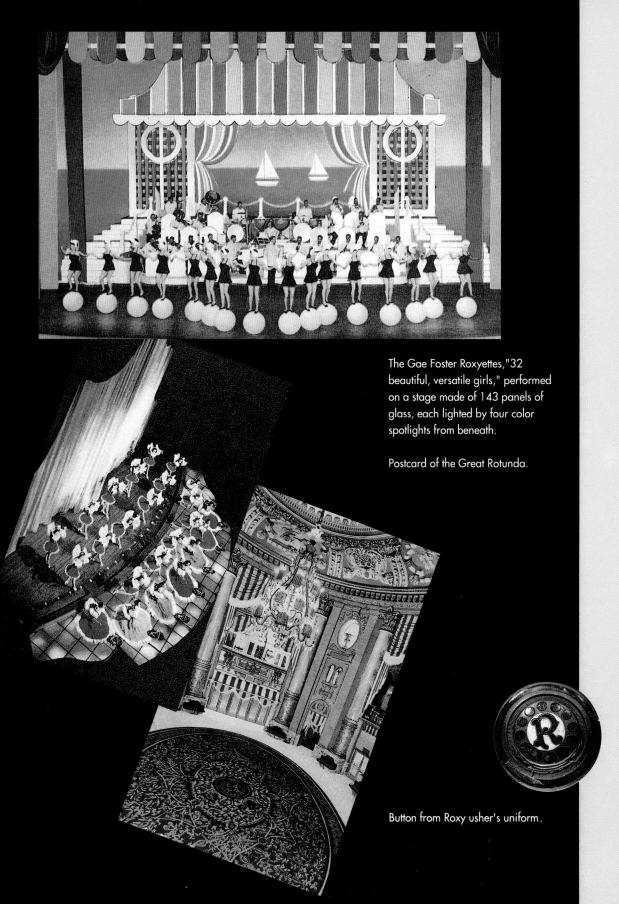

The Gae Foster Roxyettes, "32 beautiful, versatile girls," performed on a stage made of 143 panels of glass, each lighted by four color spotlights from beneath.

Postcard of the Great Rotunda.

Button from Roxy usher's uniform.

The Roxy

"Mama, does God live here?" gasped an awestruck young girl in a famous cartoon of the day as she entered the regal, five-story-high, "great bronze bowl" rotunda lobby at New York City's Roxy Theater. When this "Cathedral of the Motion Picture," as its owners billed it, opened in March of 1927, it marked the pinnacle of the era of the picture palace, as well as the climax of the career of entertainment pioneer Samuel Lionel Rothafel, the man who came to be known and loved by the world as Roxy.

From 1914 through the early 1920s, Roxy practiced and honed his visionary ideas about entertainment as a total escape in a spectacular environment while managing and revamping the Regent, the Strand, the Rialto, the Rivoli, and the Capital in New York. When the opportunity arose to build his own first-run theater from scratch, he conceived a veritable fairyland of novelty, comfort, and conveniences. For his shrine, only the sky was the limit. At Seventh Avenue and Fiftieth Street arose the theater to top them all—the Roxy. An exuberant mix of Renaissance, Gothic, and Moorish styles was concocted by architect W. W. Ahlschlager and chief designer Harold W. Rambusch. The theater boasted six box offices; 6,214 red plush seats monogrammed with an *R*; the largest oval rug in the world; bronze statues and oil paintings; a musician's gallery to serenade waiting patrons; the *Roxy Theatre Weekly Review*, a twenty-four-page take-home magazine; a staffed hospital; a miniature golf course; bowling alleys; three great golden organ consoles; the 110-piece Roxy Symphony Orchestra; a corp of dancers called the Roxyettes (precursors of the Rockettes); frankincense seeping from air-conditioning ducts; and the guardians of it all, the troupe of Roxy ushers. This elite, handpicked battalion of 125 polite, uniformed young men—trained as intensely as West Point cadets in the arts of politeness and decorum—were memorialized forever in a line from Cole Porter's "You're the Top," which extolled the steppes of Russia and the pants on a Roxy usher. (In 1960, the Roxy was demolished.)

Fox Theater postcard, St. Louis, Missouri.

Fox Theater Grand Staircase postcard, St. Louis, Missouri. The "fabulous Fox" of St. Louis, designed by C. Howard Crane in 1929, closed in 1978 but was then restored to all of its baroque Siamese splendor in the 1980s. It is now used for concerts and stage shows as well as for movies.

The Fox Village
Westwood, California

I was born in Chicago in 1950, but before my first birthday my parents moved to Los Angeles. Our house was in Westwood, the backyard butting up against the Veterans Cemetery next to UCLA. Westwood Village was not the rather loud honky-tonk place it is today. It was a sleepy little Spanish styled village with book stores, restaurants and the three movie theatres that figure so prominently in my youth: the Fox Village Theatre, the Bruin Theatre across the street, and on the other side of Wilshire on Westwood Boulevard, the Crest Theatre. They are all still there, now showing first run pictures.

The Fox Village is by far the grandest. As a kid, I often thought that the large six pointed star painted on the ceiling had some special significance. Perhaps this was a theatre especially for Jews? I remember seeing a double feature of *King Kong vs. Godzilla* and *The Day of the Triffids* there. Try as I might, I found no Jewish symbolism in either picture.

When I went with my sister to see *Journey to the Center of the Earth*, we sat in the balcony. When James Mason dropped his torch into the crater, it fell and fell finally disappearing into the darkness. This so terrified my sister Jean we had to leave.

The Crest truly looms large in my life as it was there I saw *The Seventh Voyage of Sinbad*. This is the movie that inspired me to make movies. My first true "suspension of disbelief."

Motion pictures are meant to be seen in a theatre on a big screen with an audience. A scary movie is scarier, a funny movie is funnier, when viewed with a crowd. When *Love Story* played the Fox Village, the management handed out Kleenex as you stood in line. While *The Godfather* ran there, Mario's, the Italian restaurant across the street, did huge business too.

Movie theatres are houses of magic. The magnificent movie palaces were literally cathedrals to cinema. But even the rattiest shoe box theatre in the crummiest mall can still create that special environment when the lights go down and the image hits the screen.

John Landis
Los Angeles, California

Fox Westwood Village, Westwood, Los Angeles, California. Designed in 1931 by P. O. Lewis, this Fox is in Spanish colonial style with zigzag moderne flourishes.

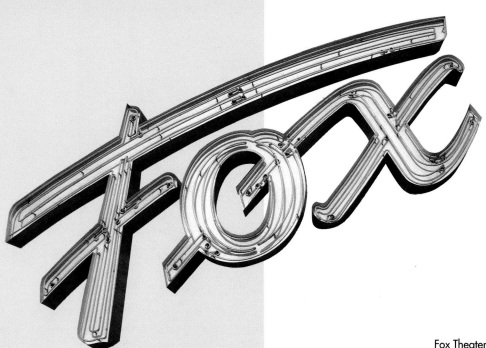

Fox Theater tower, Bakersfield, California. S. Charles Lee designed this Fox as a Spanish colonial-style theater in 1930; later it was updated by adding a streamline marquee and entrance.

The Foxes

In the old days, the major studios controlled every aspect of movie production, distribution, and display. As the end product of this process, studios built their own theaters across the country in which to show their films: movie houses named Fox (for Twentieth Century Fox), Paramount, and Warner proliferated along the Main Streets of America. This monopolistic practice came to an end in the 1950s, when a legal decision forced film production companies to divest themselves of their theater holdings. But, even now, studio names remain on the theaters. Seen here are some of the best of the Fox production numbers.

Fox Theater, Riverside, California. This Fox, designed in 1928 by Balch and Stanberry, is a Spanish colonial revival theater with arcaded walkways along the street.

Fox Theater tower, Visalia, California. This is another Spanish colonial Fox designed by Balch and Stanberry in 1928-1929. The clocks on all four sides were still in working order.

Fox Theater, Oakland, California. Designed in 1928 by Weeks and Day, this exotic theater has a tiled dome that is Far Eastern in flavor.

Fox tower, Missoula, Montana. The theater was closed, its marquee decaying, but its grand tower still loomed regally above downtown.

Fox Theater, Hutchinson, Kansas. The Hutchinson Fox, designed by the Boller Brothers, closed briefly in the 1980s. It is now being restored for use as a performing arts center.

The Warner Theater, Atlantic City, New Jersey, and postcard of the interior. An "atmospheric" with twinkling stars within, the Warner was designed by Rapp and Rapp in about 1929. The auditorium was razed years ago, but its entry facade survives as a Food & Brew restaurant sandwiched in among the enormous casinos along Atlantic City's famous boardwalk.

The Warner

Atlantic City, New Jersey

The Warner Theater on the Boardwalk in Atlantic City, N.J., opened on June 19, 1929. To a young child growing into a young adult, the Warner Theater was pure magic! The Boardwalk frontage belied the enormous lobbies and theater inside the small facade. One small entrance lobby led into a beautiful outer foyer, then into a sumptuous main lobby and finally into the amazing atmospheric auditorium. The design was Moorish, resembling a Spanish courtyard. The ceiling disappeared into a simulated blue sky with floating clouds and hundreds of stars creating an astronomically correct heaven. I had never been further away than New York City when I first started going to the Warner, but once inside I was in every foreign land I had ever read about or imagined. I gazed at the ornate iron-wrought staircases, the Carrara marble statues and the twinkling evening stars. As I sat there in awe, I was convinced that no other place on earth could ever be as beautiful as this exotic movie palace in my own hometown.

Today when I walk by the small preserved remnant of this theater, I sometimes close my eyes and recall the excitement I would feel at the mere anticipation of a visit to the Warner Theater.

Vicki Gold Levi
Co-Founder of the Atlantic City
Historical Museum
New York, New York

AUDITORIUM OF WARNER THEATRE, ATLANTIC CITY, N. J.   "WONDER THEATRE OF THE WORLD"

Mount Baker Theater in Bellingham, Washington, designed in 1927 by R. C. Reamer, is dominated by its elegant bell tower.

Mount Baker Theater box office.

The State
Portland, Maine

I grew up in Portland, Maine. I knew from the age of four that I wanted to perform. Or maybe it was my mother who knew I wanted to perform at the age of four, because I can't remember anything before my twelfth birthday. But from twelve on, the images are vivid and clear, and I think they all began at the State Theater on Congress Street, right between the Portland Public Library and a huge statue of Henry Wadsworth Longfellow reading "The Children's Hour" to three or four bronze children.

Blue Denim, a teen film starring Brandon de Wilde and Carol Lynley, was playing at the State and continued to play for seven days as I sat in the back row of the theater sort of making out with Mark Finks. I thought I was Carol Lynley, who in the movie gets pregnant by Brandon de Wilde and can't tell her parents but can tell Brandon and his friends who are playing cards in a rec room somewhere. Through lots of hugging and kissing and crying and holding each other in positions that looked great in the movies but impossible to reproduce in real life (believe me, I tried to with Mark Finks), Brandon and Carol decide she should have an abortion. She gets driven away one dark and rainy night by a sinister woman and a sinister doctor, has the abortion, almost dies, tells her parents but can never see Brandon again.

Well, I can't even remember eating my Milk Duds at the time, I was so mesmerized by the story. And it was there at the State Theater that I developed this self-righteous stance (which still persists today) that no one around me dare talk in the movies. I thought and still do think that a movie theater demands respect, much like a library. In solitude, in privacy, in silence, you can escape for a few hours into another world.

The State Theater, although it still exists today, plays only adult films: XXX rated. Mr. Longfellow is still reading to three or four small bronze children and the Public Library remains the one safe place to escape into another world.

Andrea Martin, Actress
Pacific Palisades, California

Hollywood Theater,
in Portland, Oregon,
was designed
in 1926 by Bennes
and Herzog. It
is resplendent with
its orgy of glazed
ornamentation.

63

SCENE FOUR

THEY RAN THE SHOW

Nowadays, going to the movies is a nameless, faceless, impersonal experience. But once upon a time, movie theaters were personal statements, an extension of the owners' tastes and personalities. In addition to being congenial hosts, these entrepreneurs were also profit-oriented capitalists, people who ran small and large businesses so typical of our individualistic, free-enterprise system. Off-screen, there labored an unknown cast of characters, people not listed in any on-screen credits.

A manager for forty years in central New York kept his audiences entertained in ways other than showing the movies—and he thrived on meeting and greeting many of the thousands who came through the doors of his theaters. Being an usher was more complex than it seemed. It involved not only leading people to their seats politely, but also required the talents of policeman, diplomat, and valet. A teenager from a small town in the Midwest was thrilled to land a job as a "box office girl." Not only did she get to see all the movies first and for free, but from her catbird seat smack dab in the middle of Main Street she also enjoyed the powerful advantage of being more "in the know" than anyone else in town.

"Box office girl" selling tickets circa 1940.

As our lives were shaped by what we saw at the movies, as movie stars made millions of dollars being part of the public eye, the people who worked in movie theaters across the country shaped their own careers, goals, and aspirations as they made their patrons feel right at home in front of the silver screen.

Cashier at the Nuart
Blackfoot, Idaho

Sixty years ago, February 12, 1930, the Nuart Theatre first opened its doors to the residents of Blackfoot, Idaho, and surrounding farming communities. This was the first "talking" motion picture theatre in that area. Mr. Paul DeMordaunt of Blackfoot and Mr. Hugh Drennen of Rexburg, Idaho, were the co-owners of the theatre; later, Mr. DeMordaunt purchased Mr. Drennen's interest.

Mr. DeMordaunt's widow, who still lives in Blackfoot, told me the Nuart was designed by Mr. DeMordaunt's brother, an architect, Walter DeMordaunt of Pueblo, Colorado. Walter had developed a new type of architecture, thus the name "Nuart." Walter DeMordaunt sent the plans day-by-day to the local contractor, and he did not actually see the theatre until it was completed.

In 1934, as a sophomore in high school, I started working as a cashier at the old Mission Theatre, a second-rate movie house which opened only on weekends and which was also owned by Mr. DeMordaunt. The following year, I was promoted to the Nuart as a cashier where I continued to work through my senior year.

Mr. DeMordaunt was a very distinguished-looking gentleman—tall, handsomely groomed and very strict. Any employee who chewed gum while working was promptly fired—I rarely chew gum to this day!

Many lessons were learned the hard way, but served us well in the long run. Besides, basically they were fun days of our past.

One evening, one of the ushers came to work, received his paycheck, calculated his hourly wage (which was

Nuart Theater, Blackfoot, Idaho.

9 cents an hour), walked into Mr. DeMordaunt's office, handed him his check, and said, "Here, you apparently need this more than I do," and walked off the job. I was highly paid as cashier—12 cents an hour! But, during the depression years, we were lucky to have any kind of work, so most of us stayed; besides, the surroundings were very "plush" and sometimes we forgot about the depression.

Many of the ushers who worked there during the depression later established fine careers. One became a doctor, practiced in Idaho Falls, and was Mr. DeMordaunt's personal physician for many years. He often reminded Mr. DeMordaunt of how "cheap" he was in the "old days."

For all the problems, I wouldn't change those years for anything!!

Helen K. Brown
Retired Executive Secretary
Idaho Falls, Idaho

Loyola Theater,
Los Angeles, California.
This box office is an elegant example of the "little glass room" type of ticket booth found across the country.

"Box Office Girl" at the Fox
Beatrice, Nebraska

Heaven, when I was a kid, seemed like a nice place, but a little on the boring side. Sitting around on clouds all day, squeaky clean, well-mannered, adoring God and playing the harp—not my idea of Paradise. Still, the alternative was scary. So it was that I envisioned the perfect paradise: total and unrestricted access without being locked into even "perfect happiness." I found it in the box office of the Fox Theater in Beatrice, Nebraska, in 1955.

I was fourteen and my job as "the box office girl," a position I assumed without the messy interim phase of making popcorn or selling jujubes because of my dad's friendship with the manager, was like going to heaven—without sacrificing any fun, and while being very much alive.

Cinema Centre (formerly Fox Theater), Beatrice, Nebraska.

In addition to assuming some necessary economic responsibility for the sweater sets and matching Capezio's that were as essential to me in those years as, say, breathing, my job gave me the incalculably valuable small-town advantage of being more "in the know" than anyone else.

The Fox wasn't Beatrice's only movie house, but it certainly was the best. In those days, the box office was a little glass room, more on the street than in the theatre. The rounded, three-sided window afforded excellent sightlines for tracking who was with whom, when, in what fashion (remember when the driver's seat held two?) and also gave a high probability of guessing where they were going. My hours were 6:30 to 9:00, perfect "school night" freedom from home or library, and since attendance during the week rarely hit double-digit levels, I could get some homework

done if necessary or if the traffic was light. There was a phone I didn't have to share, and my job "required" I use it.

Once I had arrived at a sort of slide rule approach to ticket costs and making change during those pre-calculator years, it was a piece of Angel Food. I could have doubled my income (55¢ an hour, $9.45 a week) had *The Beatrice Daily Sun* invited me to write a gossip column.

But, best of all were those magical hours at the movies—seeing everything first, tasting forbidden thrills from forbidden films (in pre-rating days, parental guidance was quite rigid in Beatrice), the power of granting access to friends—and the absolute Heavenly Best: being able to come in and out—in and out, and in and out, and in and out, almost without end—without having to sit through the boring parts.

Phyllis (Knipping) Gates
Magazine Executive
New York, New York

Silent Film Pianist

LILLIAN GISH
TRIANGLE STAR

In a highly technical and computerized age where machines can easily
eliminate the handcrafted product, I am what actor Eli Wallach calls
"the last of a dying breed," a silent film pianist who has tremoloed
his way across the length and breadth of the United States in "live"
performances of the classic and not-so-classic films. I have
performed in theatres, museums, high schools, church basements, and
apartments. Through the miracle of silent films, I have lived my
life vicariously in an older America, an America that never really
was. How was Richard Barthelmess able to rescue Lillian Gish from
going over the falls? What method did Buster Keaton use to
successfully steal a train and drive it through enemy lines? Did
Charlie Chaplin, in a fit of hunger, *actually* eat a shoe?

When I was fourteen years old and bored with school in Newark, I sometimes cut my tenth grade
classes and stole away to New York City on the same 107 bus that Philip Roth's Portnoy used
to ride. On one of those stolen days I had seen a listing that the Museum of Modern Art was
showing a silent film that day with *"live" piano accompaniment!* With less than a year of
playing the piano with bands at weddings, Bar Mitzvahs, and bowling banquets, I realized that
playing for the silent films might be another way of making money, spending Saturday nights
in more refined places, and meeting other people who had more than a passive interest in
films.

So I went to the Museum of Modern Art and the timing couldn't have been more fortuitous, for
sitting *alone* in one of the middle-section rows was the lady who almost went over the falls
in D. W. Griffith's *Way Down East*. Without a moment's hesitation and with all of the courage
a star-struck fourteen-year-old could muster, I sat down next to her and said, "Hello, Miss
Gish I knew who you were you were on the ice floe and here you are I want to play the piano
for silent films." I took a deep breath, and at the end of the film, Miss Gish introduced me
to the Museum's pianist, Arthur Kleiner, who in effect became my musical mentor. Miss Gish,
wonderful Miss Gish, became and remains my constant source of encouragement.

Playing the piano for the silent films is the musical equivalent of being a long distance
runner. You have to be in musical shape, able to underscore subtly every nuance, to be able
to provide the mood of the film in musical terms without overstating it. You are the constant
emotion, the conscience of the players.

Stuart Oderman
Silent Film Pianist
East Orange, New Jersey

Being a Projectionist in Colorado

I've worked, off and on, as a projectionist during the last 15 years. Mostly, I've worked in small houses where they use 16 mm equipment, but I started off right, with old non-automated 35 mm equipment, in a third-run house in Colorado. A family ran the place, and I helped out after I got off of work. It was the only theater in town, lodged in what had been the school, then a community hall. We ran three different films per week, and got some pretty good ones. That summer, I got to see *Young Winston* six times: three from the projection booth, and three from the tiny lobby, where we made the best popcorn on earth.

The problem was, since we were at the end of the distribution chain for most movies, some of our prints were pretty hacked up by the time they got to us. I think that some of the bozo splices in the prints must have been made with gaffer's tape—they were so thick, they'd jam the film transport. Usually this was no real problem—the audience expected it, they'd hoot and holler, then go buy more popcorn—and we'd clear the jam pretty quickly.

Humiliation for a projectionist is having a projector go down while running a good movie. Real humiliation is having to, in one weekend, borrow projectors from both the public library and the Episcopal cathedral in order to show a tasty example of early Nastassia Kinski cheesecake.

David Ware
Curator
Billings, Montana

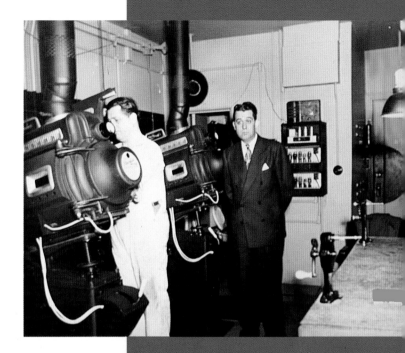

Inside a projection booth,
Capitol Theater, Grand Island, Nebraska,
mid-1930s.

Alex Theater marquee,
Glendale, California.

Charles Theater,
Charles City, Iowa.

Evangeline Theater,
New Iberia, Louisiana.

Wilma Theater,
Coeur D'Alene, Idaho.

Stanley Theater,
Utica, New York.

Ben Bolt Theater,
Chillicothe, Missouri.

May Theater,
Oklahoma City, Oklahoma.

Martin Theater,
Panama City, Florida.

Victoria Theater sign,
Victoria, Texas.

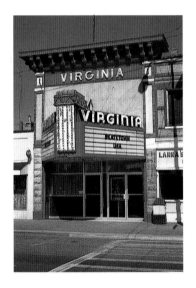

Virginia Theater,
Shelby, Idaho.

Martin Theater,
Talladega, Alabama.

The Name Game

The scenario is clear. Whether it's Roxy Rothafel opening the most famous movie palace in New York City in the 1920s or a small-town entrepreneur going into business with a more modest showcase on Main Street, USA, the answer to the question "What shall I call it?" remains the same. The nomenclature of these theaters reflects the obvious (and sometimes not so obvious) answers to this question.

Roxy named his theater after himself. The Martin family name lives atop marquees all over the Southeast. Other movie houses are named after their town, which often were themselves already named after someone— as in the Victoria in Victoria, Texas, and the Charles in Charles City, Iowa. But the Ben Bolt in Chillicothe, Missouri, opened in 1949, was the exception to the rule. "Ben Bolt" was the name of a famous nineteenth-century song written by a wandering minstrel—one Nelson Kneasse—who died in Chillicothe in 1869 and who is buried there.

71

Warner Theater,
Long Beach,
California, 1948.

Father Managed the Theater

By the time I was born, in 1948, my father had been in the theater business for 16 years. At that time he managed the old Warner Bros. Theater in downtown San Pedro, California, just up from Long Beach. He was so proud he put the announcement of my birth right up on the marquee where Bogart and Bacall were supposed to be. I took my first steps in that place and fell down the aisle and split my lip. Anyway, when I was three we moved south of Long Beach to Seal Beach, a small town on the ocean. It was there in the United Artist Theater that I spent a lot of time in the early Fifties.

My dad was always coming up with promotions involving one movie or another. *House on a Haunted Hill* had a skeleton rigged in the ceiling from one end to another on an invisible cable. Right at the scariest point in the movie he would let it loose, flying it over the customers' heads. They screamed for the rest of the picture. Once he put a full petting zoo in the lobby.

The UA itself was beautiful, deco in style with large burgundy velvet couches and huge gold light fixtures. I always thought that when I could, I would do my own house that way.

Janice Kenner Adler
Los Angeles, California

Warner Bros. Executive in the 1930s

When I think of the movies and growing up in Manhattan in the Fifties, I can't remember a single title, or the name of a single star. I do see the R.K.O. on East 86th Street, where we were dropped off on Saturday afternoon and made to sit on the far right in the children's section, patrolled by a white-uniformed matron, while skeletons descended slowly on rusty pulleys from above; or the dark blue starry Persian fairy-tale sky that enveloped me at the Loews on East 72nd Street; or standing in the bon-bon line in the Parisian sidewalk look-alike lobby of the Trans-Lux 85th Street.

At about the same time that I was hiding under my coat at the horror movies, I discovered a series of black and white photographs of my father, Beno Slesin. He had died in 1947 when I was two and one-half years old. I had already treasured his business cards, which noted his rise as a Paris-based movie executive for Warner Bros. His job included opening movie houses and distributing films throughout Europe, Africa, and eventually the Middle East—Egypt and Palestine. I was also mesmerized by the old photographs and yellowing press clippings. There he was Zelig-like—unsmiling in the Errol Flynn/Lili Damita entourage when the Hollywood stars alighted in Paris as visiting royalty. There he was in the early 1930s, behind an imposing glass-topped desk at 5, Avenue Velasquez, seated beneath three framed portraits of the Warner brothers. That was all I needed to immerse myself in the glamorous world of the movies.

Suzanne Slesin
Journalist
New York, New York

Beno Slesin, Paris, 1947.

BENO SLESIN
ASSISTANT DIRECTEUR GÉNÉRAL
POUR L'EUROPE ET L'AFRIQUE
WARNER BROS. FIRST NATIONAL FILMS, Inc.
TÉL. BUREAU: LAB. 88-52
5, AVENUE VÉLASQUEZ
PARIS (8e)

Forty Years as a Theater Manager in New York State

I was born on March 10, 1909, in Canastota, N.Y., a small Central New York village, on the banks of the Erie Canal (the film *Red Wheels Rolling* in its opening depicts this canal area). On July 14, 1914, playing on the bridge that transversed the canal, the bridge came down on my leg, severing it just below the hip. At first I maligned God for taking my leg away, but in the later years I thanked him—so many great things had happened in my life that never would have occurred if I had had two legs. And in whatever I attempted, athletically or otherwise, having one leg never proved to be a handicap, but in most cases, an asset.

One asset was that the local theater was hard put to shovel ashes out of the cellar. It did have one small window at the rear of the theater but they needed a small person to get in and out of the window. What do you know—they hired me at age six to climb in and out of that window; can you believe it?

In 1933 I was given the keys to the front door of the town's closed theater and told to "run it." After a lot of "hit and miss" I got the hang of it and my 40 years of managing and supervising started.

I always loved to meet people. Young, old, whatever—and to talk with them. I was never a wallflower. Thus becoming a movie manager was a natural. Now I had tens of thousands of folks to meet. And in the pursuit of my avocation I loved to greet my patrons as they entered the theater, and to bid them goodnight on their way out. Such an idyllic picture.

In 40 years of my theater work there was rarely a week when I didn't put on "bank nite," "dish nite," or an amateur show. One bank night I called 4 boys to come up and roll the barrel. The first one was named Robert . . . the second one was named Robert . . . I seized on this to get the audience in a lively mood . . . the third one, believe it or not, was named Robert . . . the audience was dying with laughter by this time. I called on the fourth boy, and I'll be damned if his name wasn't also Robert. I laughed so much tears came out of my eyes, and I doubt the audience ever got over the laugh stitches they got that night.

Antonio C. Balducci
Gainesville, Florida

Rivoli Theater audience, South Fallsburg, New York, 1953. Mr. Balducci hired a photographer for the showing of his first 3-D picture at the Rivoli. Upon a prearranged signal, the projectionist turned on the house lights, and this photograph was taken from the theater's stage.

Mr. Balducci poses with a Rita Hayworth poster that he created in his own sign shop at the Regent Theater, Syracuse, New York, circa 1943.

Usher's uniform sleeve, Paramount Theater,
New York, New York, circa 1950.

The Granada
Brooklyn, New York

To the kids growing up in Brooklyn, Brooklyn
wasn't a borough or even a city. It was the
whole world. We went to school in Brooklyn
and played basketball in the Brooklyn
schoolyards and football in its fields and
stickball in its streets. We congregated in
front of its candy stores and played
stoopball on its sidewalks and every Saturday
—come rain or shine or summer heat—we went
to the movies.

Our theatre was the Granada and it was
neither regal nor opulent. On Tuesday nights,
each patron would get a free dish. Wednesday
was Bingo night, so you saw two films, the
news, several shorts, a cartoon—and—you
played Bingo and could win huge amounts of
cash pyramiding all the way up to ten
dollars. At the Saturday matinees, you saw
the two features, two or three cartoons, and
a week-to-week episodic saga starring Flash
Gordon or some other more-than-heroic
character.

By 1939, I was so well known at the Granada
that I was offered a job as an usher. To be
twelve and to have both a job and a uniform
was a thrill to be exceeded only by the
experience that followed: I saw *Gunga Din*
twenty-eight times in one week. *Gunga Din*,
with Cary Grant and Douglas Fairbanks, Jr.,
and the toughest soldier in the world, Victor
McLaglen—and I saw it twenty-eight times in
one week. I lived and died with their
adventures. I laughed when they teased and
joshed each other and cried when Gunga Din,
perhaps the noblest man I'd ever known, died
to save his comrades. That week I was a
changed "man." I knew that this movie was
going to have an enormous effect on my life.
I decided then that if it were humanly
possible, I would join the British Army in
India. Of course, the next week I saw *Lost
Horizons* and became deeply interested in
becoming a Tibetan monk.

Matty Simmons
Producer
Los Angeles, California

Usher at the Manor

Pittsburgh, Pennsylvania

I believe it was 1940 when Jack Forbes, my best friend, informed me that one of the ushers at the Manor Theater had quit. At the time, I was delivering the *Pittsburgh Post Gazette* and I received one-half cent for each delivery. I was definitely interested.

The manager of the theater was Joe Blowitz. He had the reputation for being very strict and not putting up with any foolishness. After a short interview, Mr. Blowitz gave me the job. It was relatively simple—we took tickets at the door, we showed people to their seats, we changed the marquee on Saturday nights, and we cleaned out the restrooms.

The first thing was to get a uniform that fit me. The ushers' room in the balcony had a rack of used uniforms of all sizes. The pants were light blue with a black stripe down the side. The coats were dark blue with black satin lapels. We wore replaceable cardboard dickies under our coats with replaceable white collars and a black bow tie. I was issued a flashlight and told to stand at aisle two and direct people.

One evening a fashionable lady came rushing up the aisle to say to Jack that she had lost a dollar bill under her seat and couldn't find it in the dark. Jack motioned for me to come follow him. The three of us went down the aisle, which was as dark as pitch. The lady pointed out the aisle and I followed Jack into the row of seats. I watched Jack shine his flashlight around, then quick as a flash stamp his foot on the dollar bill. Jack said to the lady, "Sorry, we can't find any bill." He turned off his light and in the dark quickly scooped up the bill.

During the winter months, we would collect lost gloves, hats, and overshoes. These would be stored in the manager's office. If we needed gloves or overshoes, we'd go back there and try them on till we found something that fit.

Saturday mornings and afternoons were devoted to kids' matinees. We hated it. Mothers would drop off their kids at 9 A.M. and pick them up at 4 P.M. We were the baby sitters for hundreds of kids. The place was a mad house. Most of these kids came from fairly wealthy homes and were totally unruly. All they did was race back and forth to the drinking fountain, to the candy machines, or the restrooms. They paid little or no attention to the movie. Their fun came from running around visiting their friends or yelling at them across the theater. The worst thing about it was that there was no way to put them out. In the 40s and earlier, there was no such thing as clearing the theater after each performance. People would stroll in during the middle of the show and stay until the part where they had come in. The only time the theater was actually cleared out was at 11 P.M.

Thomas V. Scully
Editor Emeritus
St. Petersburg, Florida

Usher class at Radio City Music Hall, New York, New York, circa 1935. White-gloved usher trainees are learning the location of all 6,200 seats in the house from an instructor.

The Dakota in Yankton, South Dakota,
built as an opera house about 1900 by
D. W. Rodgers, was given an art deco
facade of ceramic tile in 1941.

SCENE FIVE
SMALL TOWN STORIES

Growing up in small town America was an insular experience. Few options for fun on a Saturday night presented themselves. Perhaps one or two movie houses were nearby, or else you could drive miles and miles to find others. Being cut off from the many cultural and recreational alternatives offered in larger places meant that the ritual of going to the movies in a small town was not only all the more significant but it was also just about the only game in town.

Glamor, mystery, and romance abounded on Main Street. A young girl from Tracy, Minnesota, remembers as much about getting dressed up and riding to town as she does about seeing the shows themselves. A youngster from rural Ohio saw Marlene Dietrich in *The Blue Angel* at least six times before she was twelve years old. Next to tornadoes and football games, movies were the biggest thrill for someone growing up in Norman, Oklahoma.

The cultural impact and the content, the life-styles and the values played out on the screen, presented a tantalizing glimpse of exotic and not so exotic places that would otherwise have been foreign to people who were raised in the middle of nowhere.

Rose Theater postcard,
southwestern Louisiana, circa 1940.

This movie house in Dishman, Washington, has a distinguished art deco tower on its facade.

The Hollywood
Tracy, Minnesota

In my mind's eye, the Hollywood Theater in Tracy, Minnesota, is always back-lit by a prairie sun from the West. It was a one-story stucco building, beige and turquoise, vaguely art deco in style. The lobby was lushly carpeted with a garish, swirling design of red and rose, an elegance otherwise unknown to a farm girl who had linoleum floors at home.

Before adolescence, I was taken to no more than ten movies. Farming in southwestern Minnesota in the 1950s allowed for few luxuries. Thus, those *rare* excursions into town to go to the Hollywood remain vividly in my mind.

The first movie I remember is *The Yearling*, Marjorie Kinnan Rawlings's poignant story of rural Florida. My sister and I couldn't sleep the night we saw it. I cried uncontrollably during the film. My dad cried too, and the next morning at breakfast we cried some more.

There followed *Lassie, Come Home*, *Cheaper by the Dozen*, *Strategic Air Command* with James Stewart, two or three Ma and Pa Kettle films, and then, the awesome thrill of seeing *The Wizard of Oz*. I still shudder when I see the Winged Monkeys.

My friends and I lived in fear of the Hollywood's manager. Tyrant and bouncer that he was, we continued to put our feet up on the seats, talk and giggle and spill drinks and popcorn. His mission in life seemed to be to prevent public displays of affection in his theater. He roamed the aisles, looking for clandestine activity. A boy's arm around his girl was enough sin to have the pair evicted.

The Hollywood never ceased being a glamorous place for me. All of the ritual involved in going to the movies had its special cachet: dressing up in a sundress with can-cans underneath, wearing more lipstick than my mom liked, the rides into town with a succession of beaus, and then, one special one, Rocky; standing in the ticket line.

The theater had two smells: popcorn and a kind of musty, damp odor. I remember that the building was often cold, but even the shivering added to the excitement, I suppose. No evening was complete without several trips to the women's lounge to apply more powder, lipstick and Evening in Paris. The makeup lights in the powder room cast a pinkish glow on our troubled complexions.

In my middle years, I remain a movie buff. Although my VCR provides endless possibilities for film-watching, an evening out at a movie still has an aura of glamour about it. That Minnesota farm girl, dreaming of romance, still lives inside me.

Barbara J. Volkmann
St. Louis, Missouri

Paramount Theater, Brattleboro, Vermont.
It was destroyed by fire in April 1991.

Window card,
New Haven, Connecticut, 1937.

Dish Night in New Rochelle, New York

In the depression days of the mid-30s, some movie theaters
attempted to increase attendance by offering free china for
certain shows. There were dishes one week, cups another,
saucers a third, etc., so that an avid movie-goer could, over
a few months, accumulate several settings . . . and it was
good china. I am not positive just which shows had this
offer, but I'm inclined to think it was the mid-week
matinees.

We lived in New Rochelle then, and my mother would sometimes
attend these shows while my brother and I were in school.
Later, at supper she reported with amusement that, as
happened every time, just at the most dramatic or romantic
scene, when the audience was most deeply caught up, there
would be several crashes as a few of the day's freebies slid
off laps onto the floor.

Edwin A. Rosenberg
Danbury, Connecticut

Latimer Theatre
Wilburton, Oklahoma

The SEVIER, De Queen, Arkansas

Both the Latimer, in Wilburton, Oklahoma, and the Sevier, in De Queen, Arkansas, were owned by Mr. K. Lee Williams. The Latimer, it was boasted, was "eastern Oklahoma's most modern theater."

Sooner Theater, Norman, Oklahoma.

The Sooner and the Boomer
Norman, Oklahoma

The Sooner was the best, but the Boomer was ok too. Together, they were as close as Norman, Oklahoma, got to movie palaces when I was growing up in the 1950s. There were a few other theaters further down Main Street, and a couple of drive-ins, one out by the Canadian River and the other on the road to Oklahoma City, but the Sooner and the Boomer were the first-run outposts of cine-mythology, there in the boonies.

The Boomer was the newer of the two. Across the street from the University of Oklahoma, its marquee and sign were rounded in fifties Moderne style. The lobby, too, was coldly contemporary.

The Sooner was my favorite theater. It stood at the top of Main Street, catty-corner from the Santa Fe depot. From the outside it was typical, rather than distinctive, of theaters in the area. From the inside, too. The lobby had a counter for popcorn, Dr. Pepper, and Milk Duds. The clocks above the exits on either side of the screen were ringed by illuminated plastic advertisements, maybe for a local mortuary.

I don't know if my mother's death when I was six had anything to do with the moviegoing habits of my youth, but I did spend a lot of Sunday afternoons by myself at the Sooner. I would go in at noon and come out at six, which was enough time to see the feature two and a half times. They would let me use the phone through the box office window to call my dad to come and pick me up. During the ride home I would recount the movie, scene by scene. I'm not sure, but I think those Saturday afternoons might have been my earliest training, not to mention the reason why I became a film critic.

Rick Chatenever
Entertainment Editor
Santa Cruz Sentinel
Santa Cruz, California

Burwell Theater,
Parkersburg, West Virginia.

The Theaters of Marietta, Ohio, and the Burwell, Parkersburg, West Virginia

There were three movie theaters in Marietta, Ohio, when I grew up. The Colony (formerly the Hippodrome) and the Putnam (named for the founding family of the town) faced each other and were located on Main Street. The Ohio was located on Second Street, the crossroads of Main Street, which led to the levee and the Ohio River. The Colony had been redone to look like a southern plantation house with pillars and balconies, and had all the first run films as well as occasional special events. The Putnam seems to have never been redecorated, had double features of Grade B movies that I loved, westerns and gritty crime features, and cost 25 cents admission until it closed in the 1960's.

It is the Ohio that I remember with nostalgia. It was the first to close, had a no-nonsense facade composed of a little black Vitrolite and a hanging marquee with the name of the show clearly visible from all directions. When I was a child the Ohio had foreign films every Wednesday night, which I attended with my mother. They were a strange and exotic lot of movies, subtitled, strangely colored, and some returned annually. I had seen *The Blue Angel* (the print, I remember, was tinted blue) at least six times by the age of twelve, when the Ohio Theater closed. I had to wait years, watching Doris Day at the Colony (now closed, but not demolished), before I could go away to college and resume my passion for complicated and deceptive blondes the likes of Marlene Dietrich. I found Monica Vitti, Jean Seberg, and Catherine Deneuve in the equivalent of the Ohio in many cities across the country . . . theaters that are always small, located on a side street and owned by somebody who loves movies, one suspects, better than money.

In the sister city to Marietta, Parkersburg, W.Va., the beautiful Burwell, built as a movie theater, has just closed and will be demolished this summer to be turned into a lot for sale. The Smoot, however, is experiencing a revival, mainly because it has a full stage and can book any travelling shows and theater events that come to the area. The public is supporting it enthusiastically.

Nancy Stout
Writer/Photographer
New York, New York

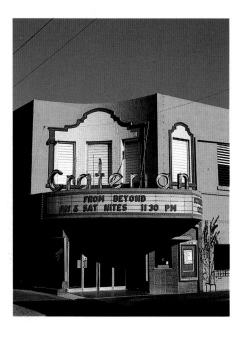

Craterian Theater, Medford, Oregon,
1942 postcard and 1987 photograph.
The sole criterion for the name of this theater
is Medford's proximity to Crater Lake National
Park. In 1942 this pun was proclaimed by
an unusual sign that spanned Central Avenue.
By 1987 the Craterian was still alive, but it
was shrinking in its own niche, having been
outmaneuvered by the cineplex theater on
the south edge of town.

The Select
Mineola, Texas

During the early 40s, my mother, sister and I were living in Mineola, a small town in East Texas. My mother had been born and reared in Mineola so we had come there to be near her family while my father, whom we called "Honey," fought the Japanese in New Guinea. I was in the first grade in 1944. We lived from weekend to weekend for the Saturday afternoon movie at the Select Theater. Admission was 9 cents for kids and 50 cents for adults. The program was always a serial with a "cliff hanger" ending, one or two cartoons and the feature. We would load up on popcorn, sodas to which we added peanuts, and Baby Ruth candy bars. We passed around toothpicks soaked in cinnamon oil and ate Kool-Aid straight from the package. The film I most vividly remember is *The Spiral Staircase*, which I still think is the scariest film ever made.

The Select Theater was half a block off Main Street and Highway 80 in between a barber shop and the office of the Jones Brothers Attorneys-at-Law. The Select served as the major stage for all the important local events. It was there, during my sophomore year in High School in 1953, that I saw my cousin Sheila crowned Queen of the Watermelon Festival.

The Select Theater was also the place where segregation was the most blatant. Blacks were only allowed to sit in the balcony, which was reached by a separate entrance on the street. After 1964 and the coming of Civil Rights, the Select could no longer legally have a "Blacks Only" section; however, as movie admissions climbed, the admission to the balcony remained 50 cents. I remember the first black couple downstairs. I remember that we tried to get in cheap by buying a ticket to the balcony which they would not sell us.

The Select Theater is still in business every weekend. The curved maroon marquee is unchanged, outlined with working white neon. I've heard they stay open by showing popular films about two months late and by selling lots of popcorn to all the school kids, black and white, who still think it's the thing to do and the place to be on Saturday afternoon.

Carol Beesley
Artist
Norman, Oklahoma

The Theaters of Sioux Falls, South Dakota

When I grew up in Sioux Falls, South Dakota, in the 1940s and 1950s, there were seven movie theaters in the city of just over 40,000 people: the State, Hollywood, Orpheum, Egyptian, Time, Dakota, and Granada. The State and the Hollywood were the most prestigious and played the best of first-run flicks. The Orpheum and Egyptian came next, offering "return engagements" of movies that had previously run at the State or Hollywood up to a year or so earlier, but sometimes showing first-runs of grade B films. The other three theaters were the Time, Dakota, and Granada. "Return engagements" of grade B pictures would be the fare at these houses.

My favorite theater was the Egyptian. It was decorated in something resembling 18th Dynasty Modern, with paintings copied from ancient Egyptian tombs and temple frescoes. It was a rather narrow theater and could never accommodate a wide screen, such as was needed for CinemaScope. The advantage of seeing films at the Egyptian was that they cost only a fraction of the price one had to pay at the State or Hollywood.

The problem with going to movies at the Orpheum or the Granada was that they attracted rowdier audiences. The Saturday matinees were especially boisterous because serials and Westerns were the prime fare and the theater was packed with kids. The noise level was incredible. I used to sit in the balcony at the Orpheum to partially escape the riot on the main floor. The balcony wasn't serene by any stretch of the imagination, but at least one didn't have to live in dread of objects such as popcorn boxes, half-filled cups of pop or other debris being dropped or thrown on you from above.

Hollywood Theater sign,
Sioux Falls, South Dakota.

I saw my first CinemaScope picture at the State Theater, which, along with the Hollywood, installed extra-wide, curved screens in the early fifties to permit the showing of these films. I saw my first 3-D movie at the Hollywood, around 1953 or 1954. It was *Fort Ti* with George Montgomery. On the same bill was a Three Stooges short, also in 3-D. For years afterward, I had the pair of special glasses handed out at the theater. They were cardboard with one lens of red plastic and the other green.

I attended all but the Time and the Dakota and infrequently, the Granada. Both the Time and the Dakota went out of business by the early 1950s. The Egyptian and the Granada were demolished about twenty years ago. The Orpheum was restored and became a community playhouse in the seventies. Recently, the Hollywood (a modern masterpiece built in 1937) closed and is slated for demolition. Of all the downtown theaters only the State remains. In the years since I have left Sioux Falls, several new theaters have been built in shopping centers or in areas away from downtown. To me, they do not have nor will ever have the atmosphere and elegance of the ones I remember from my youth.

Alan K. Lathrop
Minneapolis, Minnesota

Orpheum Theater,
Sioux Falls, South Dakota.

Egyptian Theater, De Kalb, Illnois.
The architect Elmer F. Behrens built the Egyptian in 1929. It features an elaborate glazed terra-cotta facade and a scarab stained-glass window. It was restored to its former glory in the early 1980s.

The Egyptians

Alan Lathrop fondly remembers the Egyptian Theater in Sioux Falls, South Dakota, long since gone. It was but one of a large number of Egyptian-style movie houses to be found all over the United States. They were part of a second revival of Egyptian-style architecture in America (the first took place about 1835–1840) inspired almost entirely by the breathtaking discovery of King Tut's tomb in the early 1920s. Not only was the timing of this revelation ideal to coincide with the construction of movie houses, but the contents and subject matter of King Tut's tomb were perfectly matched to the mystique of the movies. Both were romantic, exotic, and evocative of civilizations long past that have left their mark on the world.

Peery's Egyptian Theater, Ogden, Utah.
Yet another Egyptian Theater was clinging to life in the 1980s, closed, but still there. It was designed by Hodgson and McClenahan in 1924.

Grauman's Egyptian Theater postcard,
Hollywood, California. Fragments of the original
theater, designed by Meyer and Holler in 1922, still
exist today as part of a triplex, Egyptian I, II, and III.

Egyptian Theater, Boise, Idaho.
Designed in 1927 by Tourtellotte and Hummel,
this Egyptian-revival theater was lovingly restored
in the 1970s.

Hollywood Meets Main Street

Nearly every rural American town had its own movie theater. To the residents, these buildings were not small-time stories in the least. Humble Main Street pleasure domes were a unique window on the world. Movie houses were a major leisure activity for all age groups. In fact, between 1936 and 1949, the average weekly movie attendance never dropped below eighty million. The Fox Theater in McCook, Nebraska, was as important to a local resident as the Fox Westwood in Los Angeles was to filmmaker John Landis. Brattleboro, Vermont's, Paramount was as paramount in the villagers' lives as the Paramount was to sophisticated New Yorkers.

The history of any theater was a history of all theaters. Each had its own lore and legend, as well as its own cast of prototypical characters, to present the latest and greatest in motion picture entertainment. Theater managers thought up one promotion after another. Candy counter girls dispensed the goodies. Projectionists did what they could to keep the films running smoothly. People in the audience laughed and cried, cheered and booed, made out, made up, or even dozed off.

In some small towns—Grand Island, Nebraska, being an excellent example—a great amount of documentation and historical information about the movie business still exists. In Grand Island, several photographic studios document day-to-day activities, along with a longtime theater manager/owner named Wally Kemp, who diligently saved a record of his career. The entire history of movie houses everywhere took place in the microcosm of Grand Island, Nebraska.

Roxy Theater, Missoula, Montana.

Roxy Theater, Brigham City, Utah.

Sun Theater,
York, Nebraska.

Utah Theater, Logan, Utah.

Chief Theater, Pocatello, Idaho.
A porcelain enamel front and a sign depicting Indian themes dominate the facade of the Chief, designed by Walter Simon, circa 1937. It is now closed.

Nuart Theater, Moscow, Idaho.

Coronado Theater,
Lordsburg, New Mexico.

State Theater, Clovis, New Mexico.
The State has a central glass-block tower on its streamline facade.

Devon Theater, Attica, Indiana.

Al Ringling Theater,
Baraboo, Wisconsin.

Michigan Theater, Saginaw, Michigan.
The Michigan had a lustrous glass-tile
facade; the building no longer stands.

Sag Harbor Theater,
Sag Harbor, New York.

Academy Theater, Liberty, New York.
The Academy, long closed, later had its
marquee removed and then became a
furniture store, now also closed.

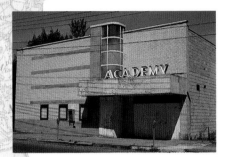

Colchester Theater, Colchester, Connecticut.
This theater's facade was the front for
an older building and was removed in
the 1980s.

Dosta Theater,
Valdosta, Georgia.

Tift Theater, Tifton, Georgia.

Crim Theater, Kilgore, Texas.
The Crim facade features the Lone Star of
Texas in glass tile as its central element.

Strand Theater, Ocean City, New Jersey.

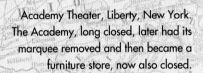

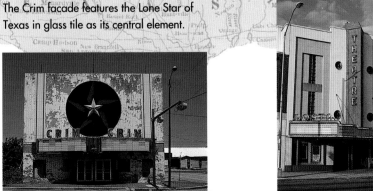

Box Offices

All of the theatricality and eccentricities of movie house architecture is boldly embodied in the frivolous and imaginative designs of the box offices, where a ticket to paradise was purchased on the way to wonderland. These extravaganzas in miniature, scaled down to the size of one person sitting behind a window, used nearly every trick in the book to beguile potential customers.

Cornell Theater,
Burbank, California.

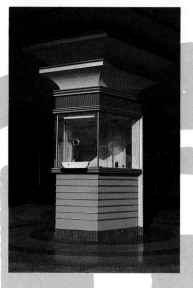

Tower Theater,
Fresno, California.

Palace Theater,
Woodbourne, New York.

Dixie Theater,
St. George, Utah.

Radio City Theater,
Ferndale, Michigan.

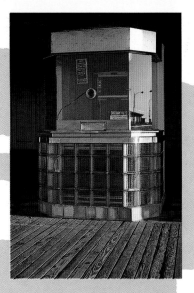

Surf Theater,
Ocean City, New Jersey.

Roxy Theater,
Caldwell, Ohio.

Ticket booths came in a dazzling variety of sizes, shapes, and colors. Some were tiny Venetian palazzi. Others were snazzy art deco production numbers straight out of Busby Berkeley. But perhaps the most appealing of all were the ones that resembled sumptuous little wedding cakes, frosted with swirls and twirls of whipped cream–like ornamentation, looking almost good enough to eat.

Freemont Theater,
San Luis Obispo, California.

Moorlyn Theater,
Ocean City, New Jersey.

Crest Theater,
Fresno, California.

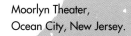

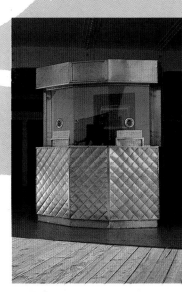

Rogue Theater,
Grants Pass, Oregon.

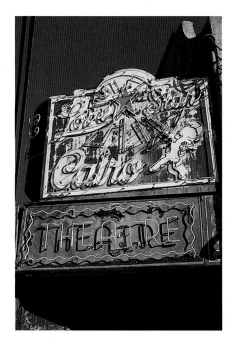

Love Star Theater,
Cairo, New York.

West Theater,
Grants, New Mexico.

The West
Northfield, Minnesota

Movies and their theaters will never be recognized
by social scientists for their profound effect on
the development of small-town American kids like
me. Unlike television, the movie house came too
early for us Saturday morning, B-movie serial
addicts to be studied and dissected by surveyors of
the passing social scene. We saw Gene Autry defeat
aliens from the center of the Earth, Flash Gordon
shoot down spacecraft flown by a new order of
Mongols, newsreels about the new order in Mongolia
and China, and sing-along cartoons where the
bouncing ball taught us about syllables and
diction.

Princess Theater,
Prosser, Washington.

Regent Theater,
Springfield, Ohio.

Lux Theater,
Grants, New Mexico.

Capitol Theater,
Aberdeen, South Dakota.

In my case, this all took place during the Korean Conflict in a little Minnesota town whose highway signs hailed Northfield as the home of "Cows, Colleges, and Contentment." Not two blocks from that midwestern brand of Madison Avenue hype was the West Theater, where two bits would admit you to a panoply of make-believe worlds. If I finished my paper route collections by 9:30 A.M. on Saturday, I could get across town before ten to squander two idyllic hours watching what would degenerate twenty years later into the G-rated, wholesome gorp that my kids watched on Saturday morning TV.

The building didn't matter, nor the sticky floors, nor the unruly company we kept. We were there to make cosmic leaps through that screen into a universe of the imagined life that was the only contentment a ten-year-old boy knew in 1951: ray guns and six-guns, good guys and bad guys, purity and pure evil. No psychologist ever probed our psyches or measured our heart rates. No sociologist traced our lifetimes for normative behaviors afflicted by images of dead Indians and murderous criminals. Why would anyone bother, when life was so simple and normal?

M. Frederic Volkmann
Vice Chancellor of Public Affairs
Washington University
St. Louis, Missouri

Posters on the sidewalk in front of the Grand Theater,
Grand Island, Nebraska, 1941.

Ingmar Bergman film at the Grand Theater,
Grand Island, Nebraska, 1964.

Hula-Hoop contest, 1958.

Grand Theater
Grand Island, Nebraska

I became an usher at the Grand Theater in 1982—oblivious as the rest of my small Nebraska town that the 50th anniversary of this once-thriving Art Deco house was passing unobserved.

I tore tickets and sold Coca Cola. Like most of the other kids on the staff, I was more interested in seeing free movies than in admiring the comic-book colored neon inside or the remains of the syrup-stained Pittsburgh Plate glass tile glass outside.

But the movies that summer—even for free—were pretty awful. And so I sat dully through one lousy film after another, three times a night, five nights a week, for twelve weeks in a row.

Eventually I stopped looking at the screen and started noticing the building around it. Thinking about it—as I had plenty of time to do.

I remembered my father telling me that he had learned of the attack on Pearl Harbor in the middle of a movie right here at the Grand. That my mother still wouldn't take a seat down front because, she said, "That's where the 'fast' girls used to sit."

Out of boredom which grew into curiosity, I explored the building from the projection booth atop it all, on down into the cellar—where I discovered a peculiar, abandoned museum of refuge.

Down there I found boxes of brittle plastic menus for 10 cent Cokes, and "Show Sold Out" signs which hadn't been needed since before I was born. I found discarded plates of the Pittsburgh glass which used to cover the theater's facade, but which had been torn down after they started popping off in the heat of the sun, bashing stray pedestrians on the head.

The biggest find for me, however, was a trivial-looking stack of old leaflets promoting a "Mother's Little Helper" Thanksgiving Day Show. A show intended to get kids out of the house while mom prepared the holiday dinner—and which I'd attended with my brother and Dad back in 1962. Free miniature pumpkin pies were served.

The sight of the faded hand-bills sent a creepy shiver down my neck, as it occurred to me that I was—at last—old enough to remember something which was gone forever. And that the plain old Grand Theater which I had taken for granted for twenty years was (good God!) some kind of historical landmark.

John Sorensen, Writer,
New York, New York

Grand Theater, Grand Island, Nebraska, opened in the spring of 1937 with a handsome blue-and-green glass-tile facade. The old tiles were replaced by more sturdy, but less flashy, blocks in the late 1970s. The theater closed in the mid-1980s, but it has recently been restored and refurbished and once again serves as a beacon for the old downtown.

The lobby, 1937.

Service station, circa 1925,
that became the Langdon Theater,
Langdon, Kansas.

Langdon Theater
Langdon, Kansas

The Langdon began life as a service station in the 1920's, and the building was converted into a theater by the early 1930's. No one can come up with the dates that this movie house was in operation, but a safe bet would be 1932 to 1942. The men who operated the theater are deceased and their families scattered and gone.

One local resident, Richard Swan, recalls that there were "jackpot" nights at the theater when a lucky patron (holding the right ticket stub) would win a $50.00 cash prize. Swan's father, who won a jackpot, applied his winnings on his first set of false teeth!

As the photo shows, the building was first used as a garage with gas pumps out front. In the picture, Charles Bellanger, garage mechanic, and Jones Holmes, service station operator (and the usual town loafers) are shown.

After the theater folded, the building became a garage again. Currently it is used for farm implements storage by a local farmer—and for storage of alfalfa hay. The building was probably constructed about 1918, at the end of World War I. The remodeling into a theater took place *about* 1931 or 1932.

Langdon, once a town of 300 persons, is no longer *needed* as a town (what with excellent highways leading to larger cities) and our population is down to 50 or 55. This is a common pattern in this part of Kansas. We'll blow away entirely one of these days.

Guilford Railsback
Langdon, Kansas

Langdon Theater, Langdon, Kansas.

SCENE SIX
SATURDAY MATINEES

The best day of the week featured the all-American childhood ritual: hour after hour of cartoons, serials, newsreels, one or two features, and sometimes even a visiting celebrity from the land of make-believe. This heady mixture was enriched by peanuts, popcorn, candy, soda pop, and the happy companionship of friends and peers. Often, the content of the show was obliterated by the high-spirited high jinks of the audience.

One universal favorite pastime was folding popcorn boxes flat and sailing them toward the screen. In rural Missouri, Tex and his Wonder Horse didn't go over too well, but a Duncan Yo-Yo demonstration was well-received in West Texas. The enchanted magic of Saturday matinees extended long after the show was over, with make-believe games and fantastic dreams.

It seemed as though the excitement and adventure of spending nearly all day lost in the semidarkness of a theater—munching, necking, and hacking around—could never ever be topped. But then, there was always next Saturday. . . .

A Saturday matinee in 1946 at the Capitol Theater, Montpelier, Vermont.

Advertising blotter.

The Lyric
Tuckahoe, New York

The Lyric Theater in Tuckahoe, N.Y., was no palace—a squat of plaster between a drugstore and a shoe store, half a block away from the village plaza. It was a controversial place, not because of the films shown (weeks after the first-run houses of White Plains and Mt. Vernon had shown them), but because of the audience.

In a moment of memorable 1930s bigotry, one of the residents of nearby Colonial Heights had renamed the Lyric the Itch, because black and Italian children who lived in Tuckahoe were in attendance, and their reputations for cleanliness, obedience and proper language never satisfied the Wasps and Jews of Colonial Heights. So the parents of those of us "on the hill" tried to persuade us to attend films in Bronxville, Scarsdale, and even Mt. Vernon. The theaters were larger, airier and more comfortable. That was true. But we preferred the Itch, even when it meant countermanding a family order.

The Itch was cheaper—10 cents, as I remember, on Saturday afternoon, compared to 25 cents in Bronxville. The Itch showed double features; the tonier houses did not. The Itch had the glamour of the forbidden. The Itch had serials—Dick Tracy, Flash Gordon and Buck Rogers. The Itch had newsreels, cartoons (Looney Tunes more beloved by our set than Mickey Mouse). It had Coming Attractions and thousands of children learned, before pubescence, that the promise of excitement could be more exciting than the event itself.

A Saturday at the Itch lasted longer than four hours. We ate Jujubes or Milky Ways, sometimes Melo-rolls, never popcorn. We sat on torn seats. Fans blew, no air-conditioning. Film tore, at least once each matinee; children booed, stamped feet and often had fist fights with other children occupying adjacent rows. Sitting up front, where you had to crane your neck, was more prestigious than sitting in the back. Horror movies were worshipped.

The architecture was forgettable, a rectangle of four walls, slightly curved to suggest aspirations of art moderne. No balcony. No center aisle. No sculpture, no cherubs or open skies on the ceiling. Stucco walls, a maroon drapery to cover the screen prior to performance. Children cheered when the drape parted and the lights dimmed. A small stage in front of the screen.

We pampered children of the hill tried not to use the bathrooms, more fear than snobbery. Even in those innocent days, kids from the town picked on kids from Colonial Heights, a primitive but effective way to battle the caste system. And bathrooms were ideal places to destroy dignity.

The Itch is gone, along with the thrill.

Art Seidenbaum
Journalist
Los Angeles, California

Grand Theater handbill,
Grand Island, Nebraska, 1942.

Candy Counter, Capitol Theater,
Grand Island, Nebraska.

Magazine advertisements, 1947.

The Crotona
Bronx, New York

My father judged a great movie house by the architectural period of the lobby and the frequency of Ritz Brothers movies.

Being a kid with a sweet tooth of elephant tusk dimensions, my endorsement turned on the variety of dental destruction offered at the candy counter.

The Crotona Theater on Tremont Avenue in the Bronx got rave reviews from any sticky-faced urchin that survived a Saturday matinee of Ma and Pa Kettle, Monte Hale, Woody Woodpecker and Spysmasher on the confections bought in the theater. The Crotona Theater had a candy counter that almost ran the entire length of the west wall of the lobby. It was serviced by two little old ladies who dressed like nurses but acted like the Brewster sisters from *Arsenic and Old Lace*.

Entering the theater I would immediately head for the candy counter to take stock of the day's bill of fare. Unlike the feeble choices found in today's movie houses, there was a time when the snack bar selections were literally overwhelming. The Crotona's menu ran along these lines: popcorn (of course), hot dogs, ice cream, soda, and an astounding array of candy.

For some perverse reason, I developed a taste for a candy bar renowned for its resistance to consumption. I refer to a gaily wrapped piece of white ceramic tile sold as Bonomo's Turkish Taffy. At first, Bonomo's offered only a vanilla version of this popular taffy; then it added a chocolate companion. Either flavor had one thing in common, neither stomach acid nor battery acid could penetrate its glistening surface. You could suck on a bar of Bonomo's taffy through two features, five cartoons, a newsreel, three chapters of a serial and a dozen coming attractions without reducing its mass in a measurable degree. In fact the only known way of ridding yourself of a bar of Bonomo's was to smack it against something equally firm (anvils were recommended), thereby shattering the taffy into mouth-size portions that could then be swallowed. I can remember stepping over dozens of discarded Turkish Taffy bars on the floor of the Crotona that looked exactly as they had when originally unwrapped and unsucked.

Had I saved my first bar of Bonomo's Turkish Taffy I'm sure I would still be pulling it over my tongue while I watched *Police Academy XII*.

Robert Versandi
Writer
New York, New York

Snack Time

Say to anyone, "Let's go to the movies," and almost immediately thoughts of popcorn, candy, and soda come to mind. It is hard to imagine movies without food concession stands. But it wasn't always so.

During the twenties, shops adjacent to majestic theaters sold food and drink that patrons consumed before or after the show. White-gloved ushers leading the way to plush velvet seats inspired awed reverence. Smacking of burlesque and the carnival, food within the picture palace was most definitely not allowed.

The economic consequences of the Great Depression, necessitating cutbacks in lavishness and services, changed the ambience at the picture show. Patrons now seated themselves, and the experience became entirely more casual. With attendance dropping, owners seeking new enticements focused on the potentially profitable lure of snacking.

First came the candy stand, stocked with myriad, prepackaged goodies. Next popcorn, a treat that was already widely available on the street, arrived in paradise. Crafty owners simply moved the vendors' carts into the lobby. Popcorn was cheap and easy to make, filling and nutritious to eat, and the aroma was completely irresistible. Popcorn production became such big business that it grew into a major farm crop during the forties. "Find a good location for a popcorn stand," the saying went, "and build a theater around it."

With the introduction of beverages—a must to wash down salty snacks—the array of temptations was complete. By the fifties, a soda machine was lodged in every movie theater lobby in America. Carefully choreographed intermissions—sandwiched between double features, cartoons, and newsreels—encouraged repeated trips to the candy counter. Watching and eating became, and still are, ritualistically and irrevocably intertwined.

Trail Drive-In Theater,
San Antonio, Texas.

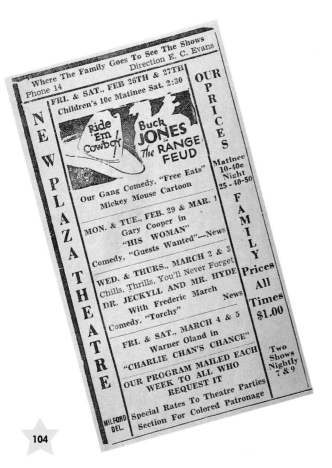

The Higginsville
Higginsville, Missouri

I never was awarded any little gold washed lapel pins for perfect Sunday School attendance but I do not think that, between the ages of six and thirteen, I ever missed a Saturday matinee. They cost a nickel. Sometimes you could buy your way in with five RC bottle caps.

My friends and I travelled in packs to and from the movie theatre for life for us was not unlike the violent, episodic cowboy, war and action/adventure 'B' movies we saw. In the late '40s and early '50s in small towns in central Missouri bloody noses, black eyes, loose teeth and torn shirts were facts of life.

Higginsville's shabby little movie theatre was owner-operated. The architecture of the movie palace in *The Last Picture Show* in Texas was scrumptious by comparison. But it was packed, standing room only, every Saturday afternoon with yelling, screaming, spit ball throwing kids like me. The main feature would be something written in blood by Republic, at least three years old. The second feature was from the theatre owner's personal collection of worn out nitrate stock films. We (and probably he) never knew ahead of time what the "selected second feature" would be.

There would be a fire in the projection booth at least once a month during the second feature. But—hey, pal, this was a time of real two fisted, stand up guys. He never called the fire department. The theatre owner, the ushers and the snack bar girl would put it out. We'd mill around outside and they'd open the doors and try to blow some of the smoke out. Then we'd go back in and see the rest of the selected feature through a haze. Often he got the reels out of order. Sometimes he would show reels from several different movies. Occasionally we weren't sure. We drew the line when he'd try to show the same second feature on successive

Saturdays. We'd stamp and yell and create meteoric showers of popcorn, pop cups, ice and little sister's shoes in the glare of the projector.

Everything was in black and white and the second feature, with a hundred splices, introduced me to the jump cut years before Godard. That I have no problem following Buñuel I owe to my early cinema education at the Higginsville Theatre. Reels of third rate film noir shown out of sequence gave me an early taste for surrealism.

Once, a real live movie star came to the Higginsville movie theatre. I think his name was Tex and although the movie we saw was forgettable, the live stage show, "Tex and His Wonder Horse," was the highlight of all my 1940s Saturday matinee adventures. After his feature ended, Tex strolled out on the tiny stage and said something like: "Well how 'bout that, little buckaroos." Then he went through some lame riddles about jackrabbits and prairie dogs. He asked for a volunteer and did a card trick. We couldn't believe it. This guy was a lot fatter than the cowboy on the screen and was treating us like we were in Sunday School.

Kids started hollering up observations about Tex's six guns (he wore a brace of them) having 26 shots without reloading. Then somebody led out "The Wonder Stallion." Clearly, it wasn't the horse in the movies. Probably it was some local farmer's nag. The saddle was a very simple thing compared to the elaborate one in the film. The critics pointed out the disparity. The horse didn't want to be on that little stage. We yelled and whistled. She started turning around and around. The theatre owner came out and led her off. "Pee, you" observed the kids in the front row. We all stood up. The horse had left a pile of "road apples" on the stage. The crowd howled.

Tex whipped out his two ivory handled, silver plated 45s and pulled off 12 absolutely deafening shots point blank at the audience. He blew the smoke from the barrels. We were in shock. We looked for signs of blood on ourselves and our buddies. There were no bullet holes in the seats. There were no jokes. It was the only quiet cinema moment of my childhood. The mechanics of blanks were not universally understood by this otherwise sophisticated audience.

My ears rang for two days so I can't be sure exactly what Tex said, but I think it was on the order of: "Did you little shit asses get them counted right?" He twirled the Colts several times, shoved them into the fancy Mexican holsters and went behind the curtain.

Leland Payton
Writer/Photographer
Springfield, Missouri

The Fort
Kearney, Nebraska

Sometime in the middle of the week the Kearney *Daily Hub* would publish the ad for the upcoming Saturday double feature at the Fort, and we couldn't wait for that ad. The Saturday double feature was one of the suns around which my particular solar system revolved from the time I was eight years old until I became much older and didn't like them anymore, at around fifteen. My friends Johnnie Martin, Bill Boyd and Georgie Downing also read the ad, of course, and if we liked the movies we would begin negotiating with our parents to let us go. The double feature wasn't the only thing to do in Kearney on a Saturday afternoon: there was also the swimming pool, making trenches in the alley, playing football (or baseball or track). But it was an important thing to do.

We would sit directly in the middle, look around a lot at who else was there, and eat popcorn. We were not much for running screaming up and down the aisles. But we didn't mind others doing it. The best fun was folding the popcorn boxes flat and sailing them toward the screen. If you were either skillful or lucky, your box would hit the screen and lodge between it and the black frame around it, so the box could still be seen, sitting there, while the movie played. I could put the box on the screen about once a month.

The first time I saw a Tarzan movie with a new Tarzan—Lex Barker or somebody like that—I was shocked. The movie was ruined, the fantasy was not the same. It was when they no longer could decide who played Tarzan that I gradually gave up Saturday afternoons at the movies.

Robert Jensen
Architect
New York, New York

Fort Theater, Kearney, Nebraska.
A close look proves that the Fort in a previous life dispensed joy as the Empress, as seen in a 1930s postcard.

West Theater, Cedartown, Georgia.
A glazed terra-cotta vision in two-tone green, the facade
depicts ample visions of the muses of drama and music.

The West
Cedartown, Georgia

It was more than just a "ticket to paradise," it was the keystone to the greatest day of my youth. It was Saturday in Cedartown, a 9,000 population center of the universe with more churches per person than any other rural town in the U.S.A.

Sundays were our parents' day of celebration, but Saturdays were the Shangri-la of seven days of anxiety, anticipation and planning. Every kid in town would meet at the West Theater at 9 A.M. for three to four hours of newsreels, cartoons, serials, double features, cherry Cokes and popcorn.

I must confess that the architecture of the West Theater left no impression. I do remember a very generous tile utilization, and I do remember huge animals that were taller than I was—unusual figures that I could just about walk into. Now that I think about it, it seems funny that I could describe the Methodist Church in the minutest detail, but at the "West"—the real chapel of hope, prayers, worship—I only recall the lady who sold the tickets behind a glass window (I thought she had rigor mortis), the old guy who took the tickets and swept the lobby, the glass candy counter containing the bullion of youth, the dark, musty cathedral of true joy, and the warm rich velvet wombs of pleasure where we slouched, wiggled and converged every Saturday of the most important time of my life. In retrospect, I really can't imagine any other more significant period of life!

The best deal of the year was once a year when we could get into the movie—usually an all-day double feature affair—by bringing some canned goods for the needy.

To this day there is nothing like the rush I get when walking by the side doors of an older theater and catching a whiff of that musty, stale smell.

Thomas Adamson
Virginia Beach, Virginia

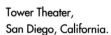

Tower Theater,
San Diego, California.

Tower Theater,
Willows, California.
The vertical tower sign
of this theater was
punctuated by "swiss
cheese" holes typical of
1950s design.

Tower Theater,
Klamath Falls, Oregon.
The Klamath Tower had
been subdivided into
four theaters—the
current trend in theater
construction. But even
that did not help to save
this art deco structure; it
closed in 1988.

Towers

The "tower" was a powerful and symbolic name for theaters across America. Along Main Street, two kinds of buildings loomed above the rest, reaching for the sky—churches and movie houses. The churches' steeples were climbing up closer to heaven; the theaters were extended above the prevailing cornice line to call extra attention to themselves because their purpose was frivolous in comparison to the necessities being sold in the downtown shops. In the 1920s and 1930s, the garish and tantalizing movie houses were trying to entice patrons to spend a dime or a quarter for a couple of hours of entertainment instead of for more down-to-earth, sensible commodities such as food and clothing.

Tower Theater,
Bend, Oregon.

Tower Theater,
Sacramento, California.

Tower Theater,
Fresno, California.
This elegant tower was
designed by S. Charles
Lee in 1940.

Tower Theater,
Oklahoma City, Oklahoma.
This tiny polychrome tower was
reduced to the indignity of
showing grade-B, R-rated fare.

The Esquire
Amarillo, Texas

I first went to the Saturday Morning Show sometime in the late 40's. I was the little brother. I was four or five. We went every week. Our mother drove, gave us each a quarter. Admission was 9 cents. Popcorn was 10 cents. This left 5 cents for a Coke and 1 cent for bubble gum which we bought next door at Cretney's Drug Store after the show.

The Esquire was huge and dark. It had a balcony that was closed on Saturday morning, even darker, distant, forbidden. When the lights came up, we could see the murals on the side walls. Giant cactus, silhouettes of cowboys on horseback all done in cafe au lait and watered down turquoise. The theatre was full of kids. You could fold the popcorn box flat and sail it high through the air. Rumor had it someone had lost an eye.

Once I remember a representative from the Duncan Yo-Yo Company coming and carving beautiful decorations on the bigger boys' yo-yos, their names, various designs, and even a tropical palm tree. The boys would get on stage and compete at yo-yo tricks for cloth patches which they wore proudly on their jackets. My oldest brother trained me to dump the remnants of popcorn, hulls, seeds, salt, on various of his girlfriends' heads. I was six. When I was twelve or thirteen, I touched the elastic band of Pat A.'s underpants in that same theatre. It was the most exciting moment of my life.

I went back in 1981 or 1982 just before the Esquire was torn down. I had lived in New York City for almost twenty years. I walked through the old neighborhood past my grade school, and went to the theatre. The final presentation before destruction was a revival of *The Sound of Music*. The theatre seemed awfully narrow. There was almost no one there. The popcorn stand was closed.

Michael Marsh
New York, New York

Esquire Theater, Amarillo, Texas.
The Esquire was designed in a blocky, zigzag moderne style.

Terrace Drive-In Theater, Bakersfield, California.
The Terrace, with its elegant art deco trim and lettering, promised a "fashionable"
evening at the cinema. The small "For Sale" sign portends a future shopping center.

SCENE SEVEN
DRIVE-INS

In the early 1930s, an ingenious movie nut from New Jersey came up with the idea of projecting flickering images from the hood of his car onto a screen. Who would have thought that this jerry-rigged invention would evolve into a multimillion-dollar industry that not only changed the viewing habits of the movie audience but also, more importantly, the anthropological behavior of three generations? Station wagons full of fun were the vehicles for close-knit family outings of childhood; the front seat of a souped-up Mercury was the arena for the first awakenings of sensual and hormonal lust.

In rural New Jersey, Mom, Dad, the kids, the kids' friends, and even the family's trusty mutt, Buster, convened in a station wagon in a parking lot for an innocent twelve-hour marathon—the dusk-to-dawner. In Amarillo, a mischievous fourteen-year-old set off a cherry bomb beneath a van that had been transformed by its occupants into a makeshift love nest. In Alabama, over the years, a bunch of kids became a pack of teenagers, as too much ice cream became too much beer.

The whole experience of the drive-in—the grade-B movies, playgrounds, snack bars, and forbidden pleasures—is an endangered way of life. The sixty-year-old fad has fallen victim to TV, VCRs, changing social mores, and the rising cost of real estate. *Sic transit gloria mundi.*

Postcard of a drive-in audience in Detroit, Michigan, in the late 1930s.

Rubidoux Drive-In Theater, Rubidoux, California. The Rubidoux displays its history on its sleeve — the old monolithic central structure clearly shows its winglike additions, appended to accommodate newer wide-format movies.

Snack bar, Orange Drive-In Theater, Orange, California, 1945.

The Ringoes
Ringoes, New Jersey

Growing up in a small rural community in the 1950s was sometimes rather wonderful. One of my fondest memories is about the Ringoes Drive-In, in a suburb of Flemington in Hunterdon County, New Jersey. Every holiday weekend in the summer the Ringoes featured an extraordinary event—Dusk to Dawn features! This meant a continual orgy of film, from sun down to sun up.

Preparing for the "Dusk to Dawn" was an elaborate ordeal. My mother (who was a very good sport about the matter) prepared snacks, dinner, beverages, sleeping stuff, damp washcloths, towels, clean, neatly-pressed P.J.'s, dog toys, aspirin, a first-aid kit—all carefully packed into shopping bags and hampers. The Bar-B-Q equipment was my father's department.

This is how it worked. After loading our Buick station wagon with all our supplies, and us, including Mom, Dad, my brother Andy, and our trusty mutt Buster, our first stop was at our neighbor's, where we picked up my two best friends, Kathy and Butchie.

We had to be in line by 5 P.M. in order to get a good spot. The first feature started at 8:45. The gates opened at 6:00. Being about tenth in line and after paying our $2.00 a car load, we would try to park as close to the screen as possible. This made it easier for Mom because she could keep an eye on us while we played on the swings and chutes beneath the giant weathered screen.

The first matter of business was starting a charcoal fire in one of the stone Bar-B-Q Pits provided for family picnics. We would have a classic holiday dinner—hot dogs and ice tea. During dinner, we would hear rumors about what was playing. The shows, which consisted of five full-length features, always had a theme. My favorite was the horror shows. My most vivid memory is of a series of films which all had the name

Dracula in the title, such chillers as *Dracula's Bride, The Revenge of Dracula, The Return of Dracula,* and *Dracula's Curse.*

As dusk approached, the excitement began to build. By now, every slot was filled with cars, pickups and people on foot (since there was no movie theater in town, this drive-in allowed walk-ins, and a bleacher with a speaker was located near the refreshment stand). Kids in sleeping bags lined up in front of the first curved row of cars. One of my Mom's first chores was to make sure everyone got a good rub-down with mosquito repellent. The ointment was then passed from car to car, since not everyone was as well prepared as we were.

Of course there was the usual on-screen welcome—cartoons, ads for local merchants, and at least three minutes about the goodies available at the refreshment stand. Then, lo and behold, the clock for the five-minute countdown flashed on the screen. Just before the final sixty seconds, the manager would announce that out of courtesy to your neighbor, it would be impolite to talk or yell loudly, and that absolute silence would be greatly appreciated. However, to let everyone get any yelling or screaming out of their system, you would be allowed to hoot, holler, scream, blow your car horn or whatever. For one minute only. What a din arose from that old corn field. People beat their fists on car doors. Dogs barked. Babies cried.

The first feature held everyone's attention. As the evening wore on (about the middle of the second film), when most of the little kids, including Butchie and Kathy, started to doze off, it was time to slip into your P.J.'s. Between the second and third film, there was a ten minute intermission. As the five-film program unfolded, the quality began to deteriorate. One of the first things you noticed was a slow but steady

exodus of cars. Occasionally a scream would be heard. Someone had pulled away with the speaker still attached to the window.

By 2 or 3 A.M. a kind of zombieish hush would settle over the remaining cars. Our cars were parked in a field, probably planted with winter rye. Sometimes a thick, damp, low fog would engulf the field. On regular non-event weekends, if the fog did obscure the screen, the manager would offer "fog checks."

At the last intermission, just before the final feature, the manager would announce half-price refreshments. It was now 4 or 5 in the morning and not many people were stirring. After the last rush for a bargain hot-dog or box of popcorn, the final exodus would start ever so slowly. If you had made it this far, why give up now, I thought. Just as the very last image on the screen disappeared, everyone would blow their horns, kind of like applause.

Jerry Harmyk
New York, New York

Vermont Drive-In Theater program, Los Angeles, California, 1948.

North 53 Drive-In Theater sign,
Rome, Georgia.

Bonholzer Drive-In Theater sign,
Washington State, circa 1965.

Drive-In Marquees

Advertising what is showing at the drive-in is a much different problem than at the movie houses downtown. On Main Street the building is in the thick of things, and the marquee tells all at a glance to pedestrians as well as to those cruising by in their cars. Drive-ins, on the other hand, are way out of town in the middle of nowhere, and as often as not, the screen ("the building") is far away from the passing parade of cars. To advertise their offerings, drive-in operators constructed signs—sometimes flashy, sometimes humble—as highway billboards to inform and attract their clientele.

Paducah Drive-In Theater sign,
Paducah, Kentucky.

Trail Drive-In Theater sign,
Sarasota-Bradenton, Florida.

Skyway Drive-In Theater sign,
Ashtabula, Ohio.

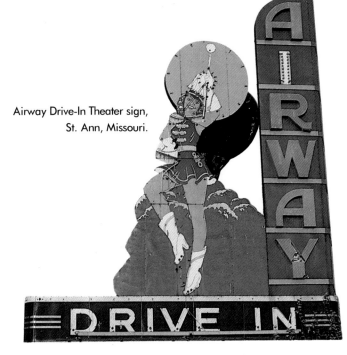

Airway Drive-In Theater sign,
St. Ann, Missouri.

Capitol Drive-In Theater sign,
Des Moines, Iowa.

Grove Drive-In Theater sign, Springdale, Arkansas.

Viking Outdoor Cinema sign,
Anderson, South Carolina.

Flamingo Drive-In Theater sign,
Hobbs, New Mexico.

117

A page from the opening program of the Olympic Drive-In, Los Angeles, California, 1945.

Airline Drive-In Theater, Houston, Texas. The Airline, long gone, used an orgy of color and flashing neon targets to attract patrons speeding by on a nearby expressway.

118

The Bama

Calhoun County, Alabama

The Bama Drive-In was set in the foothills of the Appalachian mountains. On moonlit nights it was both wonderfully romantic and wickedly scary. A huge dark blue hill towered up just behind the white-washed screen, the moonlight causing some kind of eerie, ghoulish optical aberration.

Images that stay with me: as a small child standing with brother in the back seat, Mom and Dad in the front holding hands. Later, with a pack of boys, snaking our way in darkness along the county blacktop to the Bama, we'd cross the tracks, climb up the red clay bank to sit deaf to the words, wasting away the summer nights. Six or seven ice cream seasons passed, the same boys would pack a Ford full, tasting our first sips of beer. And, finally, in one of those Fords, I learned the touch of silk stockings and soft flesh on a summer night.

The Bama Drive-In was our church, our library, it fulfilled our cultural needs. The images on the screen took us to places out of Calhoun County, Alabama, to worlds that we could not imagine in our wildest dreams. I saw *Gone with the Wind* there, and that was history. I saw, by accident, my first Fellini film—that was art. History, art, culture. Sitting in our cars, sometimes getting drunk, sometimes making out, sometimes just watching. All the time, the Bama was teaching us how to be humans on this earth. It was a rite of passage.

Years later, after we'd all gone our separate ways, the Bama closed, like most drive-ins. But whenever I visited Calhoun County I spent time at the ghost town that used to be the Bama, looking, thinking, walking.

Wayne Sides
Photographer
Florence, Alabama

Skyvue Drive-In Theater,
Dothan, Alabama.
A corrugated backing for
the screen was made flashy
by utilizing a multicolor
sunrise-sunset motif.

Drive-in theater pamphlet
cover, 1949.

Auto Theater, Muskegon, Michigan. This drive-in, looking a lot like
a monolithic piece of abstract sculpture, had been torn down by 1982.

119

Drive-in car heater
advertisement, 1963.

Pic Mosquito Repellent
advertising poster, circa 1960.

Remco Movieland
Drive-In Theater toy,
1959. This plastic
make-believe replica of
a drive-in was not as
great as it looked on
the outside of the box,
but it was still fun for
kids to imagine and
remember all of those
nights of fun.

Advertisement for TIFA pest killer.

Linda Drive-In postcard, Palatka, Florida. This panoramic bird's-eye view of a typical drive-in shows the major elements in place: the huge screen; the gigantic parking lot with its tiers of viewing locations; and the network of roads leading in, around, and out.

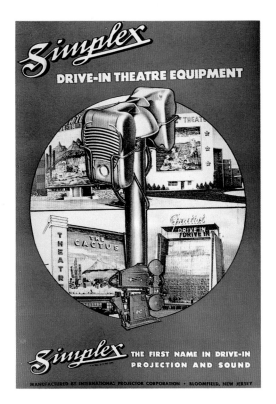

Simplex car heater advertisement.

The Drive-In Phenomenon

When the drive-in theater was "invented" in the 1930s, and as the fad caught on and multiplied after the Second World War, a whole new set of amenities and equipment evolved to serve the newest moviegoing "public"—those sitting in their cars in front of a giant screen.

Skyview Drive-In Theater,
Brockton, Massachusetts.
The ever-popular crescent moon
and stars have been pressed
into service here to create an
identity for this outdoor theater.

Rocket Drive-In Theater,
Sweetwater, Texas.
Rocket imagery was very
popular in the 1950s,
especially after the
launching of Sputnik. It
was utilized here to make
an unmemorable slab
memorable.

Harbor Drive-In Theater program, 1953,
San Diego, California.

The Starlite
Aberdeen, South Dakota

When I was five years old (1957) we moved back to Aberdeen, South
Dakota. There were one drive-in and two downtown picture houses. I
remember the Starlite Drive-In best as a child. My mother scrubbed
us clean in the tub and then dressed us in our pajamas. Then Mom
popped corn, added a great deal of butter, and tossed it in a brown
paper sack. Around sunset we all climbed into the red, '59 Chevy
with the lifetime-guaranteed, clear vinyl seat covers and headed
just west of town.

Once inside the drive-in, chunks of gravel would grind under the
wheels as Dad positioned the car up on our mound so that everyone
could see. We always chose the same spot, just a little way to the
left of the playground that was right behind the concession stand
and the projection booth. I suppose this was so my mother could
keep an eye on us.

When Dad had finished carefully adjusting the speaker on his
window, we were free to bound over to the play area with the other
children. The wonderful thing about this playground was the little
pink Ferris wheel run by an attendant in black pants and a white
shirt. There was something magical about all these kids running
around in their pajamas and circling high as the stars and the
night breeze was coming out.

The ad on the screen for the concession stand, featuring pizza that
I don't think they really had, was our cue to run back to the car.
I don't remember much about the features. I think the idea was for
us to see the cartoon and then fall asleep so my folks could watch
the show in peace. Most of the movies were poorly colored Westerns.
I do recall staying awake through *The Birdman of Alcatraz*.

We would awaken when the cars started up and honked in applause to
the film that had just ended. And we had already returned to sleep
by the time we were ushered out by men with flashlights.

Lucinda Daly, Teacher
New York, New York

Pacific Drive-In Theaters logo,
Los Angeles, California,
circa 1950.

Murals

The drive-in theater is a nonbuilding on the edge of town, facing a huge parking lot. In order to attract potential automotive patrons, drive-in operators sometimes painted huge murals on the backs of the screens facing the roads. The mural drive-ins were mostly located in Texas and Southern California. The Pacific Theater chain in California commissioned a billboard company to create these "big pictures." But what was conceived as an idea for advertising and profit also resulted in the creation of great works of street art for the automobile culture. Sadly, these bold and beautiful murals are suffering the same fate as all drive-ins: they are fading away and being demolished.

Compton Drive-In Theater,
Compton, California.

Lakewood Drive-In Theater,
Lakewood, California.

San Pedro Drive-In Theater,
San Pedro, California.

Fiesta Drive-In Theater,
Laredo, Texas.

El Monte Drive-In Theater,
El Monte, California.

Tri-City Drive-In Theater,
Loma Linda, California.

Beltline Drive-In Theater,
Grand Rapids, Michigan.

Thunderbird Drive-In Theater,
Corpus Christi, Texas.

Van Nuys Drive-In Theater,
Van Nuys, California.

Circle Drive-In Theater,
Waco, Texas.

Campus Drive-In Theater,
San Diego, California.

Twin City Drive-In Theater,
Rosenberg, Texas.

Bordertown Drive-In Theater,
Laredo, Texas.

Cherry Bowl Drive-In Theater,
Honor, Michigan.

The Trail
Amarillo, Texas

When I was fourteen years old, in 1952, I got a driver's license. It was in Amarillo, Texas. My family owned a Buick Roadmaster station wagon. It could seat eight. My parents absolutely forbade us to go to drive-in movies where the good-time girls were. So, we went.

Trail Drive-In box office, Amarillo, Texas.

One night I was at the Trail Drive-In movie with eight friends, unbeknownst to my parents, of course. A laundry van came up and parked next to us. It had big front windows, a front seat and a back area. In it were a man and a woman. They seemed really old to me. They were twenty, or maybe sixty, just old. When it got dark, the couple in the van began to do weird (sexy, we imagined) things. But first they got the speaker off the post and put it in the back window and over the back seat area.

The movie started. As we watched the movie I was nervously fingering the rubber bands on my orthodontic braces. We peeked over at the van parked next to us. The man in the front seat had a pocket flashlight out. He was kissing the woman. He flipped on this light and shined it on her. All eight of us eighth-grade fourteen-year-old boys were nervous and excited, and living on the edge.

Not opening or closing the doors, the couple in the van then crawled over the front seat into the back. He showed her the way over the seat with the flashlight. From the back seat the flashlight went on and off and we could see elbows and knees and flesh and shadowy things that looked kind of like clothes being draped over the front seat. Then the flashlight went out and the van began to rock.

In those days we carried cherry bombs with us. They were sold year-round in the filling stations. There wasn't a teenager in Amarillo worth his salt who didn't have some cherry bombs hidden in some kind of alleged explosive-proof can under the front seat of his car. Once the van began rocking, our immediate problem was getting cigarettes to make a time-delay fuse for the bomb. In those days, the police would arrest you for buying cigarettes if you were under eighteen. But, there at the Trail Drive-In we *had* to have a cigarette, so the oldest-looking one of us went to the concession stand and bought popcorn and candy and gum and got some change. Then, when no one was looking, he bought a package of cigarettes from a machine. Back in the station wagon we carefully rolled tobacco out of the cigarette and stuck the cherry bomb fuse in it. We lit the fuse cigarette. Then the guy in the back seat nearest the van, which was still rocking slowly, opened the back door of the station wagon, first carefully depressing the interior light plunger to the "off" position, and then rolled the lit cherry bomb under the van. Cool! He closed the door silently. All eight of us stared straight ahead. If a cardiologist had been there and had us all attached to the heartbeat machines, he would have found no heartbeats for the next ninety seconds.

BANG!!!!

It was a great bang. It echoed. The bomb exploded under the van and the van shook. Suddenly the flashlight was on and the light beam was jumping all over. It was pointing at the floor and the ceiling and the windows and the dashboard. One or two bodies, maybe not fully dressed, climbed over into the front seat. The van revved its motor and drove off, jerking the sound speaker, the wire and the post out of the ground, which trailed the speeding van in a cloud of dust and noise as it roared out of the drive-in with no lights on except the flashlight's beam gyrating wildly. We felt like commandoes.

I don't remember anything about the movie, but that's not important. The important thing we did in Amarillo when I was fourteen was to go to every feature at the Trail Drive-In, stalking vans.

Stanley Marsh
Amarillo, Texas

Trail Drive-In Theater, Amarillo, Texas.

Lyric Theater, Lancaster, Ohio.

SCENE EIGHT
ELEGY

The beautiful and ornate movie theaters we went to when we were growing up live on in our minds. Many of them survive as treasured landmarks, painstakingly restored to their former opulent splendor.

Nearly all the others have suffered sadder fates. An unfortunate few cling to life as porno houses. Others live hermit-crab existences as nightclubs, churches, and bowling alleys. The saddest of all stand as dying dreams, withering away on the Main Streets of America. The vast majority, however, were violently and irrevocably demolished, replaced by faceless cinder-block Cinemas I, II, III, and IV on the edges of town.

Drive-in theaters have had an even harder time. Decaying slabs and overgrown parking lots litter the borders of civilization. Others have disappeared completely, leaving no traces at all.

Palace Theater, Albany, New York, 1980, and postcard, circa 1930. Not all change is for the better. Careful scrutiny of these two versions of the Palace shows that a brutally insensitive, porcelain-enamel facade was gracelessly applied to a splendid old movie palace.

Rivoli and Rialto Theaters postcard,
New York, New York.

Rivoli Theater interior postcard, 1920.

Capitol Theater
program cover,
New York, New York,
1927.

Sheridan Theater
program cover,
New York, New York,
circa 1920.

B. F. Keith's Riverside Theater
program cover, New York,
New York, 1927.

The Theaters of New York City

The Paris Theater is closing at the end of August after forty-two years on 58th Street just west of Fifth Avenue, a theater that frequently held the sensual possibilities of Brigitte Bardot on a summer afternoon.

At this point, how can one protest? Should demonstrators organize, and swirl about for an hour or so at noon on some Tuesday? Who would understand, or care?

I would, but my modest organizational skills have diminished, and even if I were to gather together a little group of determined faces for that Tuesday rendezvous it would be something like Tahiti mobilizing, and the cause, in the face of so many other more urgent themes, would appear puny and foolish on the evening newscast silly enough to run footage.

These words, then, are my crayoned protest sign, held high above my head in the noon humidity. I protest not so much the Paris's demise, but the brutal bureaucratic erasure that has wiped away the splendid language of New York moviegoing.

My son, Adam, nearly four, and my daughter, Casey, eight, will never know the pleasures of the Little Carnegie, the Normandie, the Riviera, the Riverside, the Nemo, the Grande, the Victoria, the Beverly. Instead, they will be herded into cubicle after cubicle: the 23rd Street 3224H, the Broadway 4752R. They will be swarmed over by swift-moving packs of hundreds, departing other cubicles as they are ordered to their entrance within the Ninth Avenue Pentagon of cubicles, with six dollar boxes (small) of metallic-tasting popcorn in their arms. They will, probably by ages eight and twelve, have paid eleven dollars (of my money) for the right to enter what by then will be called simply 48369Q at 82nd and Columbus (where the Endicott bookstore once was) to view a film of sixteen decapitations that will go on sale one month later in Video 48369QV next door.

In their seats, waiting for the film to begin, Adam and Casey will be shown three previews (all rated G) of films soon to play 48369Q, including the new Schwarzenegger, *The Retina*. The sound in all twelve cubicles of 48369Q (including Adam and Casey's 69Q6) will be set at a level of a Rolling Stones concert, and the screen's curvature will be hemispheric.

Very much like New York telephone exchanges with beautiful and evocative names—Atwater, Butterfield, Monument, Spring—the movie houses (and you can forget "houses" too) of Manhattan have all but lost the poetry of the city. I would like to have been able to take my children to the Orpheum or the Symphony or the Yorktown or the Thalia, or to have told them that my office phone number was Yukon 6-7000. I am left, now, with but one or two trinkets of the past: the Sutton (though I'm told it has indecently multiplied during its summer sabbatical), and the Plaza (perhaps the loveliest New York cinema of all).

Jonathan Schwartz
New York, New York

Chehalis Theater, Chehalis, Washington, 1987. Some movie houses on Main Street have become video outlets, saying, in effect, "We have met the enemy, and they are us."

Ciné 4 Theater, Medford, Oregon, 1987.
Although this anonymous "quad" is located beside a parking lot on the southern edge of Medford, it can be found lurking all over the United States. The building has no character; it no longer needs to advertise with the design of its facade the wonders and exotic flights of fancy shown within. In fact, many "multiplex" theaters are not even within sight of passing pedestrians or automobiles. Like the drive-ins of old, the theater uses a roadside sign as its marquee.

Hollywood Dream Factory, Toledo, Ohio, 1988.
A to Z Video, St. Louis, Missouri, 1988.
The ultimate movie theater of today is the living room or bedroom in our own home, and the new theater box offices are video stores, which are sprouting up everywhere. These two, in Toledo and St. Louis, are imaginative creations that are carrying on business within old storefronts. Most video outlets are simply a small counter at a convenience store or in a supermarket.

131

Grandview Theater in 1983, Columbus, Ohio.

The Grandview
Columbus, Ohio

If they could get movie theater *aroma* in a bottle . . . take equal parts of upholstery, wooden floors, carpet, and popcorn oil; add a pinch of mold and mildew; and blend it into a perfume. Then wave the open bottle, and 1948 comes back to life! (It's claimed the only brain cells whose memory does not deteriorate are those connected to the nose.)

The Grandview smelled with the best. Being a 1926 structure, it had wood floors, plus seats of wine-colored mohair. On the walls was maroon linen with silver fleurs-de-lys. The interior had a unique feature: white, cotton coverlets on the backs of the seats.

Until its final decade (it closed in 1961), the Grandview had another eccentricity. The management franchised all concessions to a small confectionery in an adjoining storefront, conducted by two old ladies who were sisters. Rose was the one who scooped the popcorn. The other one sold the candy and the comic books. The women are remembered as a community institution. Their shop had its own bouquet, making an evening at the Grandview have a one-two punch.

As for the theater aroma, only once in recent years have I stumbled upon one any good. In Akron, stepping into the outer lobby of the suburban Highland in 1988, I got a whiff of quality.

Eric Spilker
New York, New York

Grandview Theater neon marquee, 1946.

Rose the Popcorn Lady in the confectionery
at the Grandview Theater in 1947.

Theater Renovation

Some old theaters got lucky. Local communities rescued them from oblivion and lovingly restored them, so that once again they became the snazziest buildings in town.

Warner Theater marquee, Erie, Pennsylvania, 1988.
The Warner, designed by Rapp and Rapp in 1931, closed in 1977 and reopened shortly thereafter. Its marquee proudly proclaims its important role in the "new" downtown.

Capitol Theater, Yakima, Washington, 1987. Designed by B. Marcus Priteca in 1920, the city purchased the theater in 1974, but tragically, it burned to its outer walls soon thereafter. Later rebuilt as originally designed, it reopened in 1983, to become once again the showplace of the town.

Strand Theater postcard, Shreveport, Louisiana, circa 1930.

The Strand, designed by Emile Weil and opened in 1925, has a facade now dominated by its brightly colored neon sign and its elaborate baroque dome. After a painfully slow renovation process, it reopened in 1984 as a performing arts center.

Strand Theater, 1980.

Loew's Jersey, Jersey City, New Jersey.

The Theaters of Jersey City

When I was growing up in Jersey City, New Jersey, the city behind the Statue of Liberty, the city that sees only the lady's behind, we thought we were at the center of civilization. In the 1940 census, as I remember, Jersey City, which had no bookstore, not one, was the twentieth largest city in the United States.

No books, but the Stanley on Journal Square was the largest movie theater in the country—that's what they told us. It was only later that I learned that all shopping centers were called the first in the country, or at least the state. Anyway, Journal Square did have three—count'em three—theaters of magnificent proportions. The Stanley, which seemed to be designed to resemble a piazza somewhere in Italy, with side balconies like the balcony Romeo used to call up to in Verona, with a sky ceiling complete with twinkling stars. The Loews—Lowies—across the Square was actually more luxurious, but seemed more restrained, more Protestant I thought. The State around the corner was more modern, no gilt.

They were all big time. I doubt I was the only kid who learned the facts of life in the back rows. Back in the neighborhood, we had the Strand on Fairmont Avenue—12 cents on Saturdays. The last time I saw it, the Strand was a glass store and workshop. The Stanley was a church.

But the Fillmore, seventy miles away in the town of Philipsburg, now houses a newspaper. I had something to do with that. Old theaters were a drag on the real estate market in the 1960s and the Fillmore was no exception. It was closed down when I came to Philipsburg as a young engineer. A guy named Bill Blackton wanted to start a paper and figured that with the sloping floor and seats taken out, the Fillmore was a perfect newspaper office and plant. The price for the whole thing was about $4,000. Another guy, me, wanted to get out of engineering before I hurt someone. In May of 1961, we started the *Philipsburg Free Press*, with him as a publisher and me as editor. It's still in business and the name is still up there on the marquee.

Richard Reeves
Author and Columnist
Washington, D.C.

Loew's Jersey
box office.

Former theater in Rushville, Nebraska, now turned into a place of worship.

Marty's Sky-Vu III Drive-In marquee, Jamestown, North Dakota. Sheep now graze where cars once parked.

DETROIT THEATER ORGAN CLUB

Senate Theater, Dearborn, Michigan, transformed into an organ club.

Theater Reuse

Once a movie theater has served its original function, few alternative uses can be devised to ensure any kind of future. Since these buildings were auditoriums located downtown, transforming them into houses of worship became a popular and logical next step. Drive-in theaters, even when basking in the height of their popularity, were used as well for drive-in church services.

A former theater in Webb City, Missouri, became a nightclub.

Yankton Drive-In sign, Yankton, South Dakota, invites automotive worship.

Drive-In Theater, Jacksonville Beach, Florida. This old slab became a sign for a trailer park.

Congress Theater, Palouse, Washington.

Woodbine Theater, Woodbine, Georgia.

The Majestic
Easthampton, Massachusetts

The movie-watching experience certainly has changed since I was a kid growing up in Easthampton, Mass., in the 1950s. These days if I feel the urge to watch a movie, I drive over to the video store in Enfield. I go in, browse, make my selection, walk up to the desk and show my card. The person at the desk gives me a due date. I take the video home.

Who in the fifties would have predicted that "going to the movies" would be like going to the library? Not me. If you had asked me what changes I'd make in the way Americans see themselves and their world on film, I'd have said: Don't change a thing.

Next to watching a Red Sox-Yankees game at Fenway Park, a Saturday matinee at the Majestic Theater was as good as it got. The Majestic was heaven, and the price of admission was a mere 65 cents.

The Majestic is closed now. I can't remember when I went to my last Saturday matinee there, but I do remember the last time I went to a movie at the Majestic. I was a sergeant in the Air Force and home on leave. I'd been stationed in South Carolina for a year and a half and was preparing to go overseas. The fighting in Vietnam was at its peak, but I was lucky. I was headed for England. I wasn't much older than the kid who'd made those weekly pilgrimages to view the widescreen morality plays in which everything worked out in the end.

However, a lot had changed. That was October 1969. Before the lights went out, I looked around to see if I knew anyone. The people, all adults, most older than I, were unfamiliar. That was good; I didn't want to be seen here. The lights dimmed. The seats, the walls, the people, faded to black. The only thing visible were the red neon exit signs. Then the movie came on. It was X-rated.

The Majestic had become an X-rated movie house in the late 1960s. It was no longer showing movies in which heroes in 10-gallon hats won both the day and the girl. Those days were long gone, and the Majestic had lost something. So had we all.

Terrence McCarthy
Suffield, Connecticut

Selma Drive-In Theater sign, Selma, Alabama.
This billboard-marquee on the far west side
of town looks seamy, evil, and disreputable.

Falls Theater Motor Vu sign, Great Falls, Montana.
This elegant art deco sign, with its spiffy old lettering, was all
that remained in 1988; the screen was nowhere to be seen.

Top-Hi Drive-In Theater sign,
Toppenish, Washington,
had seen better days by 1987.

This former drive-in theater screen, Merkel, Texas,
went on to become a billboard.

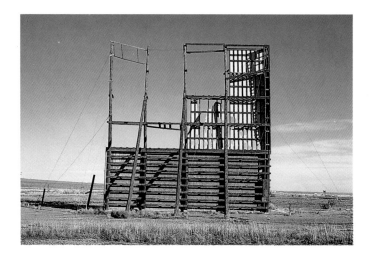

Former drive-in theater, Lordsburg,
New Mexico. Going, going, gone.

Strand Theater postcard, Seaside Park, New Jersey, circa 1935. The Strand's agonizing struggle for life is documented here. Once upon a time it was a charming theater in this resort community. At the end of its life, it had succumbed to the degradation of pornography. The Strand was torn down in the early 1980s.

Strand Theater, 1978.

The Beach

Bronx, New York

In our neighborhood, the Beach Theater on Randall Avenue lit up the block. Its bright neon lights beckoned the denizens of the project, the bungalows and Quonset huts of Classen Point, an outpost of the South Bronx on wide stretches of marshland that were still wild along Long Island Sound in the 1950's. The neighborhood was truly asleep when the lights of the Beach went out, and if we kids were still out, we knew it was bedtime.

It was always dark inside the Beach and it was often dark outside when I left, a mysterious place. I would strain to discover the outline of reality beyond the shadows and grayish walls, but never could see beyond the dim lights. But one Saturday in the early '60's, toward the end of my romance with the theater, the lights inside went on! It was the only time in hundreds of Saturdays that the house lights were bright. From behind the grime on the walls emerged peeling blue or green paint and ornate relief designs. On the ceiling, a huge, intricately designed plaster chandelier. It was almost a portent of things to come, as though it were time for the theater to reveal itself: for time was short.

At that point I was a teenager, and whether it was girls or the confusion following the explosion of the Kennedy assassination and its aftermath, I lost interest in the movies and stopped hanging out at the Beach.

Then, one day, I suddenly noticed that the marquee of the Beach was blank. For a while it stayed that way and then it read, "Closed for Renovations." The renovations never came, and a Pentacosta Iglesia claimed the space. Truly the curtain had come down on the last picture show, and there were to be no more movies at the Beach.

Ron Chomiw
Bronx, New York

Starlite Drive-In Theater sign, Bay City, Michigan.

EXIT

Selected Bibliography

The primary sources in the field of movie theater architecture are David Naylor's *American Picture Palaces: The Architecture of Fantasy* (New York: Van Nostrand Reinhold, 1981) and *Great American Movie Theaters* (Washington, D.C.: Preservation Press, National Trust for Historic Preservation, 1987). A few of the many other sources include:

Barsam, Richard Meran. *In the Dark: A Primer for the Movies.* New York: Viking Press, 1977.

Chase, Linda. *Hollywood on Main Street: The Movie House Paintings of Davis Cone.* Woodstock, N.Y.: Overlook Press, 1988.

Colombo, John Robert. *Popcorn in Paradise: The Wit and Wisdom of Hollywood.* New York: Holt, Rinehart & Winston, A Jonathan James Book, 1979.

Friedrich, Otto. *City of Nets: A Portrait of Hollywood in the 1940s.* New York: Harper & Row, 1986.

Gabler, Neal. *An Empire of Their Own: How the Jews Invented Hollywood.* New York: Crown, 1988.

Gebhard, David, et al. *A Guide to Architecture in San Francisco and Northern California.* Santa Barbara and Salt Lake City: Peregrine Smith, 1973.

Gebhard, David, and Robert Winter. *A Guide to Architecture in Los Angeles and Southern California.* Santa Barbara and Salt Lake City: Peregrine Smith, 1977.

Hall, Ben M. *The Best Remaining Seats: The Golden Age of the Movie Palace.* Revised Edition. New York: De Capo Press, 1975.

Knight, Arthur. *The Liveliest Art: A Panoramic History of the Movies.* New York: A Mentor Book, 1959.

Liebs, Chester H. *Main Street to Miracle Mile: American Roadside Architecture.* Boston: New York Graphic Society, 1985.

Maddex, Diane. *Built in the U.S.A.* Washington, D.C.: National Trust for Historic Preservation, 1985.

Mast, Gerald. *A Short History of the Movies.* Indianapolis and New York: Bobbs-Merrill Company, 1971.

Miller, Mark Crispin; ed. *Seeing Through Movies.* New York: Pantheon Books, 1990.

Percy, Walker. *The Moviegoer.* New York: Alfred A. Knopf, 1961.

Possi, Jack. *Theater in America: The Impact of Economic Forces.* Ithaca, N.Y.: Cornell University Press, 1968.

Preddy, Jane. *Glitz, Glamour and Sparkle: The Deco Theatres of John Eberson.* Chicago: Theatre Historical Society of America, 1989.

Sklar, Robert. *Movie-Make America: How the Movies Changed American Life.* New York: Random House, 1975.

John Sorensen. *Our Show Houses: The History of Movie Theaters in Grand Island, Nebraska.* The Hall County Historical Society Press; P.O. Box 1683, Grand Island, Nebraska 68802; 1990.

Illustration Credits

Unless otherwise noted here, all postcards and other ephemeral materials are from the authors' collections and photographs are by John Margolies.

9   David Crockett Theater postcard: Don Preziosi

11   Fairmount Theater postcard: Gotham Book Mart Collection

13   Theatorium postcard: Gotham Book Mart Collection

13   General Theater chain postcard: Gotham Book Mart Collection

14   Frontispiece, Western Electric Company catalog: The American Museum of the Moving Image/IATSE Collection

16   "The Reward of a new Entertainment," Western Electric Company catalog: The American Museum of the Moving Image/IATSE Collection

16   Theda Bara postcard: Gotham Book Mart Collection

17   Promotion postcard: Gotham Book Mart Collection

18   Grand Riviera: Courtesy Max Protetch Gallery, New York

20   Advertisement: From *Motion Picture Herald* (1951); Eric Spilker

21   *Frankenstein* promotion: Eric Spilker

21   Cover of brochure: The American Museum of the Moving Image/Gift of Bruce Sanders

25   "Movies" series of postcards: Gotham Book Mart Collection

28   Moviefan Family postcard: Gotham Book Mart Collection

32   Capitol Theater postcard: Seymour Durst

36   Airdome Theater postcard: Gotham Book Mart Collection

38   Douglas Fairbanks postcard: Gotham Book Mart Collection

38   Bijou Theater postcard (black and white): Gotham Book Mart Collection

39   Play at the Palm Theater: Gotham Book Mart Collection

40   Telegram postcard: Gotham Book Mart Collection

44   "Keep It Dark" postcard: Gotham Book Mart Collection

45   Strand Theater lobby: Seymour Durst

49   Pennant: Paula Rubenstein

50   Grauman's Chinese Theater postcard: Gotham Book Mart Collection

54   Roxy Theater matchbook, circa 1927: The American Museum of the Moving Image/Gift of William Savoy

55   Roxyettes postcard (horizontal): Seymour Durst

55   Roxyettes postcard (vertical): Gotham Book Mart Collection

55   Roxy usher's button: The American Museum of the Moving Image/Gift of William Savoy

List of Featured Movie Theaters

Page numbers in italics refer to illustrations.

Overleaf: Shrewsbury Drive-in Theater, Shrewsbury, Massachusetts, 1984.